THE SACRED ART OF LOVEMAKING

THROUGH THE EYES OF GOD

BY
OLGA TOMASZEWSKI

Table of Contents

The Sacred Flame Within

In the quiet sanctuary of her being, there exists a sacred flame—a divine spark placed by the Creator Himself. This flame is not merely a source of physical pleasure; it is the embodiment of life's creative force, the intersection where the physical and spiritual realms converge.

Ancient traditions recognize this sacred center within woman as the yoni, a Sanskrit term meaning "source" or "womb." It symbolizes the origin of all creation, the gateway through which life enters the world. The yoni is revered not just as an anatomical feature but as a spiritual portal, a space of profound power and mystery.

This sacred space is designed to be awakened not through force or mere physicality but through reverence, love, and deep spiritual connection.

When approached with honor and intention, it becomes a wellspring of joy, healing, and divine communion. In the union of lovers Who honor this sacredness, pleasure transcends the physical and becomes a form Of worship— a dance Of energies that mirrors the cosmic interplay of the universe. Such intimacy is not about conquest but about mutual surrender, where both partners experience a glimpse of the divine.

Embracing this understanding transforms lovemaking into a sacred act, a celebration of the divine feminine and masculine energies within us. It invites us to experience intimacy not just as a physical connection but as a spiritual journey toward wholeness and unity.

Chapter 1
The Divine Blueprint of Love-Making

The Sacred Art of Love-Making: Through the Eyes of God Introduction: Love-Making as God Intended

Before the world distorted intimacy, before love-making became separated from its sacred origin, it was designed by God to be a divine act, a reflection of His love, and a merging of two souls into a unity that mirrors the holiness of creation itself.

Love-making was never meant to be just physical pleasure, an instinct, or an earthly desire. It was intended to be a moment where two beings, created in God's image, would come together in deep connection, mind, body, and spirit, as an act of worship, surrender, and divine love.

But over time, the world has lost sight of this truth.

Intimacy has been reduced to a transaction instead of a transformation.

Love-making has become about taking instead of giving, lust instead of devotion, and self- indulgence instead of sacred unity.

Yet, God's original design has never changed.

True intimacy still has the power to heal, elevate, transform, and reflect the depth of divine love.

This chapter is the beginning of returning to that truth, reclaiming love-making as God intended, honoring it as a sacred art, and understanding how intimacy, when guided by God's love, can become the most powerful form of connection two souls can share.

The Divine Blueprint: Why God Created Love-Making Before we can explore how to practice the art of divine love-making, we must first understand why God created it.

Love-making was designed with three sacred purposes:

1 Love-Making as an Act of Divine Creation From the very beginning, God created man and woman to be co-creators with Him. Intimacy is not only the means by which life is brought into the world but also a reflection of God's power to create, to bring forth new life, and to unite two souls in a bond that mirrors His eternal love.

Genesis 1:27 (ESV) is: "So God created man in His own image, in the image of God He created him; male and female He created them."

When two people come together in love, they are not just joining bodies. They are participating in the divine act of creation. Whether it is the creation of a child, the creation of a deeper bond, or the creation of spiritual growth, love-making carries the sacred energy of life itself.

2. Love-Making as a Reflection of God's Love Intimacy between two people was never meant to be separate from God; it was meant to mirror His love for us.

"Husbands love their wives, just as Christ loved the church and gave himself up for her. Ephesians 5:25"

This scripture reveals that love-making, in its purest form, is about selfless giving, devotion, and deep connection. It is not just about receiving pleasure but about offering oneself fully, openly, and without fear, just as Christ offered Himself to us.

When love-making is approached with the heart of God's love, it becomes more than just a moment of intimacy. It becomes a sacred offering, an act of deep trust, and a reflection of divine love in human form.

3. Love-Making as the Merging of Two Souls From the very beginning, love was designed to be more than just physical; it was meant to be a complete uniting of two people in body, mind, and spirit.

Genesis 2:24 (ESV): "Therefore a man shall leave his father and his mother and hold fast to his wife, and they shall become one flesh."

One flesh does not simply mean physical unity. It means becoming one in every way. It is a merging of souls, a bond that is beyond temporary attraction, and a sacred act that ties two spirits together in divine love.

True intimacy isn't just about bodies; it's about energies, emotions, and souls becoming aligned.

This is why love-making without love leaves emptiness. Because without the presence of God, without spiritual unity, and without emotional depth, intimacy becomes nothing more than an act of the flesh lacking the true power of divine connection.

Returning to Sacred Intimacy: Reclaiming Love-Making as a Divine Act Now that we understand why God created intimacy, we must ask:

How do we return love-making to its sacred form?

How do we shift from worldly intimacy to divine intimacy?

How do we invite God into our love-making so that it reflects His highest love?

The answer is simple yet profound:

We must approach love-making not as a physical urge but as a spiritual experience.

We must see our partner as God's creation.

We must enter intimacy with reverence, not just desire.

We must make love in a way that honors God, slowly, intentionally, and fully present.

This requires a shift in mindset, a reawakening of the soul, and a commitment to making love not just as an act but as an offering.

Reflection Questions

At the end of each chapter, take a moment to reflect on these questions:

Do I see love-making as a sacred act, or has the world influenced my view of it? How can I bring more of God's presence into my understanding of intimacy?

Do I see my partner's body as something to take or as something to honor?

Have I ever experienced love-making as a moment of true connection, or has it been purely physical?

A Closing Prayer for Divine Love-Making

Lord, I desire to understand intimacy through Your eyes. I ask You to cleanse my mind of worldly distortions and help me return to the sacred purpose of love. Teach me to love with devotion, to connect beyond the physical, and to honor intimacy as You designed it to be. May my love reflect Your love, pure, whole, and filled with truth.

Amen.

NEXT CHAPTER PREVIEW:

Preparing for Sacred Love-Making

In Chapter 2, we will explore:

How to purify the heart before intimacy.

Why emotional and spiritual preparation is essential. How God wants us to prepare for a sacred union.

Final Thought: This is Just the Beginning

This chapter sets the foundation, but this book is a journey that restores, heals, and transforms intimacy into something greater than the world has ever known.

The art of love-making through God's love is an awakening, a remembrance, a return home to the deepest connection we were meant to experience.

Chapter 2
Love as Christ Loves The Foundation of Sacred Intimacy

"Husbands, love your wives, just as Christ loved the church and gave himself up for her." Ephesians 5:25

The Love That Transcends All Understanding

What does it mean to love as Christ loves?

What does it mean for a husband to love his wife in a way that reflects the deep, selfless, sacrificial love of Jesus?

This scripture from Ephesians 5:25 holds the key to sacred intimacy. It reveals that true love-making is not about power, not about possession, and not about personal fulfillment it is about giving oneself completely, as Christ gave Himself for us.

The world teaches love-making as something to be taken, but God teaches it as something to be given.

True intimacy is not found in the physical alone. It is found in a heart that loves without condition, a soul that gives without hesitation, and a union that mirrors the greatest love of all.

If a man is to love his wife as Christ loves the church, what does that mean for their intimacy?

How can their love-making reflect that divine love?

How does this change the way we prepare for, engage in, and honor intimacy?

This chapter will answer these questions, revealing how God's greatest act of love serves as the model for the deepest, most sacred form of connection between two souls.

What Does It Mean to Love as Christ Loves?

To understand love-making as an act of divine love, we must first understand the kind of love that Jesus demonstrated.

When Jesus gave Himself for the church, He loved in a way that was:

Selfless: He gave everything without expecting anything in return. Sacrificial: He laid down His life for the ones He loved.

Unwavering: His love was constant, no matter the cost.

Tender and Patient: He guided, nurtured, and cared for His people with gentleness. He devoted his love; it was not temporary but eternal.

If this is the model of love that a husband is called to give, intimacy is not about control, dominance, or fulfillment of personal needs.

Instead, it becomes:

A gift rather than a demand.

A place of safety rather than expectation.

A holy experience rather than a physical act.

This kind of love-making transcends the physical; it touches the soul, heals, nourishes, and deepens the spiritual bond between two people.

The Role of Selflessness in Love-Making

Most people enter intimacy thinking about what they will receive. But divine love is about what you are willing to give.

This is where the heart of Christ-like love transforms intimacy:

Instead of seeking pleasure first, seek connection first.

Instead of thinking about personal satisfaction, think about your partner's heart, mind, and spirit.

Instead of moving from desire alone, move from love, devotion, and surrender.

Christ's love was never about self-indulgence; it was always about giving Himself fully.

This is why true intimacy is not about the body alone. It is about love in a way that mirrors God's love, a love that nourishes, protects, and brings peace to the soul.

Sacrificial Love: The Ultimate Offering in Intimacy

"Greater love has no one than this: to lay down one's life for one's friends." John 15:13

Sacrificial love does not mean pain or suffering; it means always putting love first.

A husband loving his wife as Christ loves the church means he lays down his ego, expectations, and selfish desires. He lives in a way that makes her feel safe, seen, cherished, and adored.

In intimacy, this means:

Creating a space of emotional safety.

Being fully present, without rushing or expectation. Honoring the experience, not treating it as routine.

Seeing intimacy as an opportunity to serve, not just receive.

When love-making is approached with sacrificial love, it ceases to be about fulfilling a duty or giving in to passion. It becomes an act of devotion, an offering of selfless love, a reflection of Christ's heart.

Tenderness & Patience: The Key to Spiritual Intimacy

Jesus's love was never rushed.

It was never forceful.

It was never demanding.

Instead, His love was patient, tender, and deeply present.

In love-making, this means:

Moving slowly, letting connection be the focus, not urgency. Being present and loving with attention, not distraction.

Holding, touching, and cherishing are acts of devotion.

The world teaches us that intimacy is about intensity, passion, and conquest.

But true, Christ-like love teaches us that intimacy is about presence, tenderness, and complete surrender.

When a husband loves his wife with this kind of patience, this kind of tenderness, love- making becomes a moment of divine connection, where time disappears, and only love remains.

Devotion: Making Love Last Beyond the Bedroom

The love of Christ never wavered.

It did not come and go based on feelings.

It was a love that remained steady, constant, and eternal.

In intimacy, this means:

Love-making is not just a physical moment it is the way you speak, the way you hold each other, the way you cherish your partner outside of the bedroom.

Sacred intimacy is built long before the physical act begins; it is woven into daily life through kindness, deep conversation, and emotional closeness.

Sexual love-making without emotional and spiritual intimacy is shallow, but when the foundation of love is built daily, the act of intimacy becomes a reflection of something deeper, something divine.

At the end of each chapter, take a moment to reflect on these questions:

Do I approach intimacy with a giving heart, or do I focus on what I receive? In what ways can I practice selfless love, both in and outside of intimacy? Do I make my partner feel safe, cherished, and honored through my love? How can I bring more patience, tenderness, and devotion into my intimacy?

Final Thought:

Love-Making as an Act of Worship To love as Christ loves is not just a lesson. It is the highest calling.

When love-making is approached through the eyes of God, it ceases to be about passion alone, and it becomes a divine act, a sacred experience, a moment of complete surrender to love.

Chapter 3
The Foundation of Sacred Intimacy

Recognizing and Building Divine Love Before Love-Making Begins the Knowing: Recognizing Sacred Intimacy Before It Begins

Before two souls ever come together in the act of love-making, there is a knowing a recognition that what exists between them is different, deeper, and more sacred than anything they've encountered before.

This knowing is not just attraction, not just chemistry, not just desire.

It is a connection that feels eternal, as if their souls have met before, as if something divine is being awakened within them.

For some, this sacred bond is recognized long before physical intimacy begins. There is a deep peace, an undeniable sense of trust, and an unspoken understanding that love-making will be a spiritual experience, not just a physical one.

But for others, this depth of intimacy must be built over time, cultivated through emotional closeness, spiritual connection, and a shared commitment to something greater than themselves.

So, the question is:

Can sacred intimacy be known before love-making?

Or is it something that must be nurtured, developed, and strengthened before it is fully realized?

The answer is both.

For some, the connection is immediate, as if it was always meant to be.

For others, the foundation must be built, step by step, with patience, intention, and a willingness to create something that reflects divine love.

In this chapter, we will explore:

How to recognize a love that is truly sacred.

The signs that indicate love-making will be a deeply spiritual experience. How to build this kind of connection, even if it does not exist fully yet?

The Signs of a Sacred Connection Before Love-Making

Before intimacy begins, there are indicators signs that reveal whether a relationship has the potential to be more than physical, more than fleeting, more than the world's idea of love.

Here are the signs that indicate a love built for sacred intimacy:

A Sense of Deep Spiritual Recognition You feel as if you know each other beyond this lifetime. Your souls feel connected, even without words.

There is a divine familiarity as if you were created to find each other.

This kind of love is not something that can be forced. It simply exists.

"Before I formed you in the womb, I knew you Jeremiah 1:5"

If love-making is to be sacred, it must be built on something that feels eternal, not temporary.

A Love That Is Rooted in Emotional Safety

You feel fully seen, fully understood, and fully accepted. There is no fear of judgment, only deep trust and openness.

You do not need to hide parts of yourself or pretend to be anything other than who you are.

True intimacy cannot exist without emotional safety.

If a person makes you feel like you must earn their love, prove your worth, or chase their attention, the foundation for sacred love-making is not yet there.

"There is no fear in love, but perfect love casts out fear. John 4:18"

A Desire to Give: Not Just Receive The relationship is not about taking. It is about offering love freely. There is no sense of ownership, control, or expectation.

Each person is focused on honoring, cherishing, and uplifting the other.

The Sacred Union of Two Virgins—Love-Making Through God's Eyes In the eyes of God, the union of two souls in love-making is not just a physical act—it is a sacred ceremony, a divine merging, a moment where heaven touches earth. When two come together for the first time, their intimacy is pure, come together untainted by past experiences, free from worldly expectations.

God sees this moment not as a loss of innocence but as a passage into a deeper, holier love. It is the unfolding of a covenant, where two bodies, two hearts, and two spirits are joined in the way He intended—with reverence, tenderness, and divine presence.

1. The Beauty of First Union—A Holy Offering The first act of love-making is not just the merging of bodies—it is a gift, an offering, a sacred initiation into oneness.

✓ It is pure, untouched by the world's distortions of intimacy.

✓ It is gentle, unfolding in God's perfect timing.

✓ It is filled with awe, wonder, and the holiness of divine connection.

"Therefore, a man shall leave his father and mother and be joined to his wife, and the two shall become one flesh." Genesis 2:24

In this moment, love is not about performance, but presence. It is about feeling, discovering, and surrendering to the sacred rhythm of love.

2. The Divine Merging—Two Souls Becoming One As their bodies meet, something far greater is happening—their spirits are intertwining, their energies aligning, their very essence becoming one.

✓ Their breath synchronizes, creating a rhythm beyond time.

✓ Their touch carries the purity of devotion, not the weight of expectation.

✓ Their hearts beat as one, echoing the eternal love of their Creator.

This is not about lust or desire—it is about connection, surrender, and divine presence.

Love-making, in its truest form, is not about taking—it is about giving, offering oneself fully, freely, and with reverence.

3. The Presence of God in Sacred Intimacy God is not absent at this moment—He is there, blessing this union, covering it with divine grace.

✓ He is in the way their hands find each other, steady and reassuring.

✓ He is in the whispers, the soft sighs, the quiet wonder between them.

✓ He is in the stillness afterward, where love lingers beyond touch.

There is no shame here, no fear—only the knowledge that this act was always meant to be holy.

"Every good and perfect gift is from above." James 1:17

4. The First Surrender—Letting Go & Trusting Love For two to come together for the first time, this moment carries both excitement and vulnerability. There is an unknown, an unfolding, a letting go.

✓ She surrenders into love, knowing she is safe, cherished, and held.

✓ He enters with devotion, not seeking to take but to honor.

✓ They both give freely, knowing that love is not just a moment—it is a covenant.

Sacred love-making is not about control—it is about trust. Trusting each other, trusting the body, and trusting God's design for love.

5. After the Union—The Sacred Stillness After love has been made, there is a quiet holiness that remains. No words are needed— only presence.

✓ They lay together, wrapped in the warmth of something eternal.

✓ Their spirits are intertwined, now forever connected.

✓ A new chapter of love has begun—one built on God's foundation.

This moment is not just the end of innocence—it is the beginning of divine intimacy. It is the first step into a love that will deepen, evolve, and reflect God's eternal design.

Love was always meant to be sacred. Let it be honored, cherished, and held as the divine gift it is.

6. A Prayer for the First Union

Heavenly Father,

Let this union be pure,

Not just in body but in spirit. Let this love be holy,

A reflection of Your eternal devotion.

May their first embrace be filled with reverence, may their love-making be wrapped in divine grace,

May their souls forever be bound in Your perfect design. Bless their journey, their love, and their sacred intimacy, so that every touch, every breath, every heartbeat Is an offering of love back to You.

Amen.

Final Thought—The Sacredness of First Love

• Love-making is not meant to be rushed, taken, or treated
  as casual—it is a divine unfolding, a sacred first step
  into oneness.

For two to experience their first time is not just a
physical initiation—it is a spiritual covenant, blessed and
held in God's hands.

In God's eyes, love is always meant to be sacred,
tender, and filled with the presence of the divine.

This is not just the first act of intimacy—it is the
beginning of a lifelong, soul-deep connection.

Sacred love-making is not an act of possession. It is an
act of devotion. It is about giving without demand, without
ego, without selfishness.

"Love does not insist on its own way; it is not irritable
or resentful. Corinthians" 13:5

If both partners enter intimacy with a willingness to
give love fully, not just receive pleasure, their connection
has the potential to be truly divine.

The Presence of Patience and Emotional Maturity

You feel no rush, only a desire to grow in love at the
right pace.

There is an understanding that true love cannot be
forced; it must unfold naturally. Both partners are

committed to emotional depth, communication, and spiritual growth.

A relationship that is built with patience rather than urgency will create the strongest foundation for intimacy.

"Be completely humble and gentle; be patient, bearing with one another in love. Ephesians 4:2"

Patience reveals true love because love that is meant to last forever is never in a hurry.

A Shared Spiritual Alignment you both see love as something sacred, not just physical. There is a mutual desire to invite God into your relationship.

Love-making is seen as an act of worship, not just an act of passion.

"Do two walks together unless they have agreed to do so? Amos 3:3"

If two people are not spiritually aligned, intimacy will always feel incomplete.

But when love is centered on God, trust, and divine purpose, intimacy will reflect something far greater than the physical; it will be a union of souls.

Can Sacred Intimacy Be Built?

Not everyone recognizes divine love from the beginning.

For some, love starts as something simple, but it grows, it deepens, it strengthens, and it becomes sacred through intention, devotion, and commitment.

Even if you do not yet feel the depth of spiritual intimacy, it can be cultivated. Here's how:

Create a foundation of trust before physical intimacy begins.

Learn to speak the language of love beyond words through presence, touch, and deep listening.

Pray together and invite God into your love.

Move with patience; sacred intimacy is not rushed. See your partner as a soul first, not just a body.

If two people are willing to build this kind of love, then sacred intimacy can be achieved even if it was not there from the start.

The key is intention.

When two souls choose to honor love, nurture it, and elevate it, intimacy will naturally become sacred.

"Love bears all things, believes all things, hopes all things, endures all things. Corinthians 13:7"

Reflection Questions

Before moving forward, reflect on these questions:

Do I feel that my connection with my partner is built on something sacred? Do I feel emotionally safe, fully seen, and unconditionally loved?

Am I willing to build deeper intimacy through patience and trust? How can I invite God more deeply into my love life?

Final Thought:

Sacred Love Begins Before Love-Making Sacred intimacy is not just about the moment of connection, and it is about everything that leads to it.

It is in the way you love, the way you trust, the way you honor each other long before your bodies ever meet.

If love is built with devotion, patience, and divine purpose, then love-making will be a reflection of something eternal, something holy, something created by God.

A Closing Prayer for Divine Love

Lord, I ask for wisdom in love. I desire to experience intimacy as You designed its reflection of divine unity, a moment of complete surrender to love. Guide my heart to recognize sacred love when it appears, and if I am meant to build it, give me the patience to nurture it. Let my love be pure, my connection be honest, and my intimacy be a place where You are present.

Amen.

NEXT CHAPTER PREVIEW

Chapter 4 Preparing for Sacred Love-Making
In Chapter 4, we will explore:

How to purify the heart before intimacy.

The importance of emotional and spiritual preparation.
How God calls us to prepare for divine union.

Chapter 4
Preparing the Heart for Sacred Love-Making

Purifying the Mind, Body, and Spirit Before Intimacy: The Sacred Preparation for Love-Making

Before two souls come together in divine intimacy, there must be a preparation, an internal cleansing, a quieting of the mind, and a deep surrender of the heart.

Sacred love-making is not rushed, not careless, not simply an act of the body. It is an intentional merging of energies, an offering of love in its highest form.

Just as a temple is prepared before worship, just as a sacred space is cleansed before prayer, so too must the heart, mind, and body be prepared before intimacy.

How do we purify ourselves before love-making?

What steps must we take to enter intimacy with reverence and devotion?

How can we ensure that our love-making is aligned with God's design rather than driven by worldly desire?

This chapter will explore the spiritual preparation for intimacy, the process of aligning the heart with divine love, so that love-making becomes an act of worship, not just passion.

Purifying the Heart: Releasing Emotional Barriers to Intimacy True intimacy begins not in the body but in the heart.

Before love-making, the heart must be cleansed of fear, doubt, resentment, and emotional wounds.

If love-making is to be sacred, the heart must be Open, not guarded.

Soft, not hardened.

Present, not distracted by past pain.

This means:

Forgiving past hurts, letting go of emotional wounds that block true connection. Releasing fears, fear of vulnerability, fear of rejection, fear of not being enough. Healing from past intimate wounds so that love-making is not shadowed by old pain.

"Create in me a clean heart, O God, and renew a right spirit within me. Psalm 51:10"

A heart that is free of emotional burdens can fully experience love-making as it was meant to be pure, open, and deeply connected.

Purifying the Mind: Letting Go of Worldly Conditioning The world has distorted intimacy.

It has turned love-making into a transaction, a conquest, a temporary pleasure rather than a divine act of love.

Before entering intimacy, the mind must be cleansed of these distortions.

This means:

Letting goes of false beliefs about love and desire. Rejecting the idea that intimacy is only physical.

Releasing shame, guilt, or fear that has been placed on intimacy by past experiences or society.

"Do not conform to the pattern of this world, but be transformed by the renewing of your mind. "Romans 12:2

When the mind is clear, intimacy is no longer shallow. It becomes profound, meaningful, and deeply sacred.

Purifying the Body: Honoring the Physical Vessel

The body is not just flesh. It is a temple, a sacred vessel that holds divine energy.

Before love-making, the body must be honored, prepared, and treated with reverence.

This means:

Cleansing rituals bathing with intention, as if preparing for a sacred ceremony. Touching with love, seeing the body as holy rather than merely physical.

Nourishing the body by eating foods that sustain life, moving the body in ways that create energy and vitality.

"Do you not know that your bodies are temples of the Holy Spirit, who is in you, whom you have received from God?" 1 Corinthians 6:19

When the body is treated as a temple, love-making becomes a divine experience rather than just an act.

Spiritual Preparation: Inviting God into Intimacy

Sacred love-making is not just between two people. It is an act that involves the presence of God.

Before intimacy, the spirit must be aligned with divine love.

This can be done through:

Prayer Before Intimacy, Asking God to bless the union, to make the love pure, to align the moment with His will.

Speaking Words of Love, Whispering affirmations, devotions, and blessings over one another.

Creating a Sacred Space, lighting candles, playing soft music, making the environment peaceful and inviting.

Setting an Intention for Love-Making, rather than approaching intimacy casually, entering it with the purpose of deepening connection, honoring love, and merging souls.

"Where two or three gather in My name, there I am with them." Matthew 18:20

When God is invited into intimacy, love-making becomes more than an act, it becomes an experience of divine unity.

Signs That You Are Ready for Sacred Intimacy How do you know if you and your partner are prepared for love-making that is sacred, not just physical?

Here are the signs:

You feel emotionally safe with one another.

There is no pressure, no expectation, only love. You trust each other deeply, beyond words.

There is a sense of peace rather than urgency.

You feel that intimacy will strengthen your bond rather than fill a void. You are fully present in the moment, without distraction.

You are both spiritually aligned, desiring to honor each other in love.

If these signs are present, then love-making will be a reflection of divine love rather than just a physical experience.

Reflection Questions

Do I feel emotionally, mentally, and spiritually ready for intimacy? Have I released past wounds that may affect my ability to love freely? How can I honor my body, mind, and soul before entering love-making? What does inviting God into intimacy look like for me and my partner?

Final Thought:

Intimacy Begins Before the Physical Act Sacred love-making does not begin in the moment the bodies meet. It begins in the way two souls prepare.

When love is approached with intention, reverence, and divine presence, intimacy becomes something eternal, something transformative, something truly sacred.

NEXT CHAPTER PREVIEW:

The Art of Merging, Becoming One in Spirit, Mind, and Body

In Chapter 5, we will explore:

How intimacy is more than physical; it is a merging of souls.

The role of energy, emotion, and spiritual presence in love-making. The divine mystery of becoming one flesh in God's design.

Chapter 5
The Art of Merging: Becoming One in Spirit, Mind, and Body

The Divine Mystery of One Flesh in God Design the Sacred Act of Merging True intimacy is more than a physical act. It is the merging of two souls, the blending of energies, and the surrender of self into something greater.

The world teaches that intimacy is only about passion, pleasure, or connection between two bodies.

But in its highest form, love-making is about becoming one not just in flesh but in mind and spirit.

The phrase one flesh carries a deeper spiritual meaning. It is not just about physical closeness. It is about:

The merging of two hearts into one rhythm.

The blending of two energies into one force of love.

The surrendering of the individual self into a divine unity.

When intimacy is approached with sacred intention, it becomes a spiritual fusion, a holy act of love, a reflection of divine creation.

This chapter will explore:

How intimacy is more than physical, it is a merging of souls.

The role of energy, emotion, and spiritual presence in love-making. The divine mystery of becoming one flesh as God intended.

Beyond the Physical: Merging in Spirit

Before love-making happens in the body, it must happen in the spirit.

When two souls are deeply connected, intimacy becomes a sacred exchange, a conversation beyond words, a prayer between two bodies.

In this state:

You feel deeply seen without needing to explain yourself.

There is no fear, no shame, no holding back, only trusts and openness.

The moment becomes timeless love-making is no longer about time, only presence. Every breath, every movement, every touch feels like a form of devotion.

This is what it means to merge spiritually before merging physically.

Whoever is united with the Lord is one with Him in spirit." 1 Corinthians 6:17

If we are united with God in spirit, then true love-making must also reflect that same divine unity, one that is not rooted in the body alone but in something much greater.

Beyond the Physical: Merging in Mind & Emotion Love-making is not just about the body. It is about deep emotional connection, mental alignment, and an unbreakable bond of trust.

A true merging happens when two people are fully present, not just physically but mentally and emotionally.

Signs of mental and emotional merging in intimacy:

You feel fully present, not lost in thoughts or distractions.

You are both giving and receiving love equally, without imbalance. You feel emotionally safe and able to be vulnerable without fear.

When your minds are attuned to one another, you sense what the other feels without needing words.

When the mind and heart are deeply connected, love-making becomes a sacred conversation between two souls.

"Let the words of my mouth and the meditation of my heart be acceptable in your sight, O Lord." Psalm 19:14

Sacred intimacy is not just about what happens in the body. It is about the meditation of the heart, the alignment of the mind, and the surrendering of two souls into one love.

The Physical Merging: Becoming One Flesh in God Design

God's design for love-making is not simply about passion. It is about divine unity.

When two bodies come together in sacred intimacy, it is not just an act. It is a reflection of the way God unites His people in love.

"But he who is joined to the Lord becomes one spirit with Him." 1 Corinthians 6:17

This means that just as we are united with God in spirit, we are meant to be united with our partner in the same way.

Sacred love-making is:

A merging of energies: your body responds not just to physical sensation but to love itself. A divine surrender where ego falls away and love takes over.

A holy act is not just about pleasure but also about deep connection and divine unity.

When love-making is approached with reverence, presence, and an open heart, it ceases to be just physical; it becomes an act of divine creation and an experience of true oneness.

The Energy of Sacred Love-Making Beyond what we can see, intimacy is an exchange of energy.

When two people come together in love, they are not just touching bodies. They are exchanging life force, emotions, and spiritual energy.

"The two shall become one flesh." Mark 10:8 This one flesh is more than just a union. It is an intertwining of souls. The energy of love-making stays long after the moment is over.

This is why sacred intimacy is so powerful. It creates A lasting bond, even beyond physical presence.

A sense of deep fulfillment and emotional nourishment.

A feeling of unity that lingers long after the bodies' part.

When love-making is not just physical but spiritual, the energy exchange becomes a prayer, a sacred offering, a merging of two souls into one divine frequency.

Reflection Questions

Do I approach love-making as a merging of souls or just a physical act? How can I prepare my heart, mind, and spirit for deeper intimacy?

Am I fully present in moments of intimacy, or do distractions pull me away?

How can I invite God into my intimate connection so that it becomes a reflection of divine love?

A Closing Prayer for Sacred Merging

Lord, let my love be a reflection of Yours. Let my body, mind, and soul be fully present in love, not just for passion, but for deep connection. May my love-making be pure, honoring, and filled with Your divine presence. May I merge with my partner in a way that reflects Your unity, a love that is whole, deep, and eternal. Amen.

NEXT CHAPTER PREVIEW:

In Chapter 6 we will explore:
Recognizing Sacred Love.

Chapter 6
Recognizing Sacred Love Seeing Love Through Divine Eyes

Love is more than emotion, attraction, or companionship. Sacred love is a divine force, a spiritual connection that transcends the physical world. It is a bond felt in the soul, recognized in the heart, and guided by something greater than ourselves.

To truly experience the depth of sacred love, one must first recognize it is not just in a partner but in the way, love moves, unfolds, and reveals itself as part of a divine plan.

This chapter explores:

How to recognize when love is truly sacred.

The difference between ordinary connection and divine union. Signs that you have found a love that is meant to last eternally.

1. What Makes Love Sacred?

Many experience love, but not all experience sacred love. The difference lies in the depth of connection, the spiritual alignment, and the divine purpose behind the union.

A sacred love is not just felt. It is known. It carries a sense of destiny, purpose, and spiritual awakening.

Sacred Love Is Recognized By:

A Deep Inner Knowing. From the moment you meet, there is a recognition, a familiarity, a feeling that you have met before.

Effortless Alignment. You do not have to force the connection; it flows, it fits, and it moves with divine ease.

Mutual Spiritual Growth.

This love does not distract you from your path; instead, it aligns you with your highest self.

A Connection Beyond the Physical. The attraction is undeniable, but what binds you is deeper than the body. It is soul, mind, and spirit.

Divine Timing & Synchronicities Signs, dreams, or divine moments confirm that this love is meant to be.

A sacred love is not just about how someone makes you feel. It is about who you become in their presence.

2. Recognizing the Difference Between Sacred Love & Ordinary Love

Not all love is meant to last, and not all connections are sacred. Some are lessons, some are temporary, and some prepare you for the one that is divinely designed for you.

Ordinary Love:

Is based on attraction and compatibility but lacks deep spiritual alignment. Often requires forcing, fixing, or chasing to keep it alive.

Can feel conditional love is given based on circumstances, not essence. May be passionate but lacks deep peace, a rollercoaster of emotions.

Sacred Love:

Feels destined, as if souls were always meant to meet. Does not require chasing. It unfolds naturally.

Brings a sense of peace, even in its intensity.

Deepens both partners spiritually, leading them closer to God, self-awareness, and truth. Survive challenges because it is built on something eternal.

Sacred love is not just about being with someone you love; it is about being with someone who is part of your divine purpose.

3. The Signs That You Have Found Sacred Love

Not all love is easy, but sacred love carries signs that confirm its divine origin.

1. Your Souls Speak the Same Language You feel deeply understood, even in silence.

Communication flows without struggle, even in difficult moments. You are not afraid to be fully seen, raw, and vulnerable.

2. The Connection Feels Familiar as if You've Known Each Other Before

There is an unexplainable recognition when you meet.

The energy between you is both new and ancient at the same time. It feels as if your souls have been reunited after lifetimes apart.

3. The Relationship Is Built on More Than Physical Desire Passion is present, but what binds you is much deeper.

Your love-making is not just about pleasure. It is about connection, merging, and spiritual union.

Even in moments of stillness, you feel connected.

4. You Challenge & Inspire Each Other to Grow Spiritually. This love awakens something higher within you.

You push each other to become the best version of yourselves.

You help each other stay on the divine path rather than distracting from it.

5. Even Through Challenges, Love Remains Unshaken

Disagreements do not destroy the connection. They strengthen understanding. Love is not based on perfection but on commitment, trust, and divine timing. No matter what happens, there is a knowing that this love is meant to be.

Sacred love is not perfect, but it is eternal. It weathers storms because it is guided by something greater than human desire.

4. The Ritual of Recognition. Opening Your Eyes to Sacred Love

If you want to recognize sacred love when it appears, you must be willing to see love through divine eyes.

Practice: The Sacred Love Reflection

1. Sit in a quiet space, close your eyes, and breathe deeply.

2. Ask your heart: Have I experienced sacred love, or have I only known temporary love?

3. Reflect on past relationships. What was missing?

4. If you are in a relationship now, ask yourself:

Does this love elevate me spiritually?

Do I feel peace in my soul when I think of them?

Is this love helping me become who I am meant to be?

5. If seeking sacred love, speak this affirmation:

Open my heart to divine love. I trust that the one meant for me will be revealed in divine timing.

This ritual helps clear illusions of false love and allows you to see what is real, what is sacred, and what is meant for eternity.

The Final Thought Sacred Love is a Divine Gift

Sacred love does not leave you questioning; it confirms itself through peace and knowing. It is not bound by time, distance, or challenge. It is built on the divine foundation.

When you recognize sacred love, cherish it, honor it, and nurture it, for it is rare, precious, and part of a greater divine plan.

Love that is sacred is not just between two people. It is a reflection of God's love; an eternal promises a bond that transcends lifetimes.

To become one flesh is not just an act. It is an experience of unity, surrender, and sacred devotion.

When love-making is approached with spiritual awareness, it ceases to be ordinary, it becomes a divine encounter, a moment of true merging, a glimpse into the love that God designed for us.

A Closing Prayer for Sacred Preparation

Lord, prepare my heart for love. Let my mind be clear, my body be honored, and my spirit be aligned with Your will. Let intimacy be more than passion. Let it be a reflection of divine love. Help me to enter a sacred union with purity, presence, and reverence so that my love is a gift, not just an act. Bless this connection, and let it be a reflection of You.

Amen.

Chapter 7
The Rhythm of Love Understanding the Cycles of Intimacy

Embracing the Divine Flow of Passion, Rest, and Renewal the Sacred Timing of Love

Love, like everything in creation, moves in cycles and rhythms.

There are moments of passion and intensity, and there are moments of quiet and rest.

Just as the earth experiences seasons, intimacy follows its own natural flow is a rhythm that aligns with the body, the emotions, and the soul.

"To everything, there is a season and a time to every purpose under heaven." Ecclesiastes 3:1

Sacred intimacy is not about constantly seeking heightened passion; it is about honoring the natural rhythms of connection, energy, and renewal.

In this chapter, we will explore:

The cycles of intimacy understanding when to give and when to receive. How energy, emotions, and life seasons influence love-making.

The divine balance between passion, rest, and renewal in relationships.

By understanding the rhythm of love, we can experience intimacy that is not forced but flows naturally, deeply, and divinely.

The Cycles of Intimacy: Passion, Connection, and Rest

In every relationship, there are different phases of intimacy: moments of fire, moments of deep emotional connection, and moments of quiet reflection.

Understanding these cycles allows us to navigate love with grace, patience, and divine awareness.

The Season of Passion, Fire & Desire

This is the phase where love feels electric, intense, and deeply physical.

There is an undeniable magnetism between partners.

Desire is heightened, and love-making feels urgent and all-consuming.

Touch, closeness, and connection feel effortless and instinctive.

This is a sacred season where two souls burn brightly together, experiencing intimacy in its most heightened state.

"Love burns like blazing fire, like a mighty flame."
Song of Solomon 8:6

This is a time to surrender to passion, to explore the depth of physical connection, and to express love in its most radiant form.

However, like fire, passion must be honored with balance.

If we try to force passion constantly, it loses its sacred power. When passion naturally shifts, we must allow the rhythm of love to flow into the next phase.

The Season of Deep Connection Soulful Intimacy. After the fire of passion, love deepens into something even more profound. This is when intimacy shifts from intensity to deep emotional closeness.

Words, eye contact, and silent presence become more powerful than touch alone.

Partners feel fully seen, fully known, and fully embraced in spirit. This is the season where love transcends the physical and moves into a space of deep bonding, trust, and heart connection.

"I found the one my heart loves." Song of Solomon 3:4

This is a time to nurture the relationship beyond the body to hold space for vulnerability, to build emotional security, and to strengthen the foundation of love.

When this phase is honored, passion becomes richer, more meaningful, and more connected.

The Season of Rest and Silence, Renewal, and Reflection

There will be times when love asks for stillness, quiet, and space to breathe.

This is not a time of disconnection; it is a time of renewal. Love-making may take a gentler form through simple touch, presence, or companionship. The relationship moves into a phase of reflection, gratitude, and deep spiritual awareness.

This season mirrors nature itself, just as the earth rests in winter before blooming again in spring. Intimacy also needs moments of stillness before passion reignites.

"Be still, and know that I am God." Psalm 46:10

This is a time to trust the process of love, knowing that passion and deep connection will return when the heart is ready.

In a world that constantly pushes for more, for excitement, for constant stimulation, it is vital to recognize that love is not meant to be forced. It is meant to flow.

By honoring these seasons, we allow intimacy to flourish naturally rather than trying to control its course.

How to Align with the Natural Rhythm of Intimacy.

Now that we understand the seasons of love, how do we align ourselves with this sacred rhythm?

Listen to the Body & Soul

The body and spirit always give signals about what they need. If there is a pull toward passion, embrace it with openness and devotion. If there is a desire for deeper conversation and soul connection, lean into emotional closeness. If there is a need for rest, allow stillness and reflection without fear. By tuning in, love-making becomes an act of intuition, not expectation.

"Trust in the Lord with all your heart and lean not on your own understanding." Proverbs 3:5

When we trust the natural flow of intimacy, love deepens in ways beyond imagination. Honor the Changing Energy of Love

Intimacy does not have to look the same every time. Love-making can be fiery one day and tender the next.

There is no right way, only what feels aligned at the moment. Instead of forcing passion, chasing intensity, or fearing quiet moments, embrace the ebb and flow of love with trust and surrender.

"He has made everything beautiful in its time." Ecclesiastes 3:11

Sacred love-making is not about performance; it is about presence. Communicate & Align with Your Partner

The more two people understand their rhythms together, the deeper their intimacy will be. Have open conversations about your emotional and physical needs.

Recognize when one partner desires closeness and when the other needs space. Respect each other's timing, knowing that love flows differently for each person.

"Do everything in love." 1 Corinthians 16:14

When love is approached with patience, understanding, and divine awareness, intimacy becomes a dance of harmony and deep connection.

Reflection Questions

What season of intimacy am I in right now

Do I honor the natural rhythm of love, or do I try to control it? How can I align more deeply with the flow of my relationship?

How can I create space for passion, connection, and renewal in my love life?

A Closing Prayer for Love Divine Rhythm

Lord, let me honor the natural flow of love. Let me embrace the seasons of passion, the depth of connection, and the renewal of rest. Help me trust that love is not meant to be forced but to be received, cherished, and nurtured in Your divine timing. May my love- making be in harmony with the rhythm You created.

Amen.

NEXT CHAPTER PREVIEW:

The Power of Touch, the Language of Love Beyond Words in Chapter 8, we will explore the sacred meaning of touch in intimacy. How to use touch to express love, devotion, and presence. The divine energy exchange that happens through a physical connection.

Final Thought:

Love is a Dance of Seasons Love is not meant to stay in one phase forever it is meant to move, to shift, to evolve.

By honoring the rhythm of intimacy, we allow love to be pure, natural, and deeply fulfilling.

Chapter 8
The Power of Touch the Language of Love Beyond Words

The Sacred Meaning of Physical Connection

Touch: The Silent Prayer of Love

Long before words were spoken, before love was ever written in poetry or song, there was touch.

A hand on the heart, a gentle embrace, the warmth of skin against skin a touch has always been the purest form of communication.

It is through touch that we:

Comfort and heal

Express love without needing words. Merge energy, creating a sacred exchange.

True intimacy is not just about physical closeness. It is about presence, intention, and the ability to express love through the hands, the fingertips, and the very breath.

"They are no longer two, but one flesh." Matthew 19:6

To touch with love is to speak the language of the soul, to communicate something deeper than words could ever express.

In this chapter, we will explore the sacred meaning of touch in intimacy

How to use touch to express love, devotion, and presence. The divine energy exchange that happens through physical connection The Divine Gift of Touch In the Bible, touch is often associated with healing, blessing, and divine connection. Jesus touched the sick, and they were healed.

He blessed them through the laying of hands on them, and they were healed.

"He took the children in His arms, placed His hands on them, and blessed them." Mark 10:16

This shows us that touch is not merely physical. It carries power, meaning, and spiritual energy.

When given with pure intention, it has the ability to heal, restore, and create profound connections. A soft caress can ease the weight of the world. A strong embrace can say, you are safe with me. A lingering touch can whisper, I see you, I feel you, I love you.

To touch with presence and devotion is to make love a sacred act, beyond words, beyond time, beyond the body itself.

The Language of Touch in Love-Making Touch in sacred intimacy is not about taking. It is about giving.

It is a moment of worship, devotion, and surrender to love itself. A kiss placed with intention is a blessing. A hand on the chest is a vow of presence. The intertwining of fingers is a prayer of unity. When love-making is approached with this awareness, every touch becomes an act of divine connection.

"His left arm is under my head, and his right arm embraces me." Song of Solomon 2:6

To touch with reverence is to honor the soul of your partner, not just their body.

In sacred intimacy, the body is not just flesh; it is the vessel of the spirit. Every touch should be given with presence, not distraction. An offering of love, not a demand for pleasure. A prayer, not just a physical act.

The Energy of Touch: A Divine Exchange Beyond what we see, touch is an exchange of energy. When two people connect through an intentional, loving touch, their energy fields merge, creating a sacred flow.

The palms of the hands hold energy centers that transfer warmth, emotion, and love.

The chest and heart radiate the frequency of love and devotion. The lips carry the power of breath, of whispering love into existence.

When love-making is approached with spiritual awareness, touch becomes an act of creation. It is a moment where two souls unite not just in body, but in energy, in vibration, in divine presence.

Touch is where love meets the physical world. It is where passion meets purpose. It is where the soul speaks without needing words.

"Whoever touches you touches the apple of His eye."
Zechariah 2:8

To touch with love is to honor God's creation, to honor love itself.

How to Deepen Intimacy Through Touch

To make touch a sacred experience, practice these intentional ways of connecting: Touch with Presence. When you hold someone, be fully there. Let go of distractions, let go of thoughts, let your presence be your gift.

Even a simple touch on the shoulder, if done with awareness, can carry deep meaning.

"I have found the one whom my soul loves." Song of Solomon 3:4

Practice: The next time you touch your partner, pause. Close your eyes. Feel the warmth of their skin. Be present in the moment. Touch with Intention. Touch is not about routine. It is about meaning.

Before placing your hands on your partner, set an intention: May this touch bring peace.

May this touch remind you that you are loved. May this touch connect our souls beyond the physical. Practice: Try tracing slow, meaningful patterns on your partner's skin, as if writing a love letter without words.

Use Breath & Stillness. Sometimes, the most powerful touch is stillness. Holding each other without movement, just feeling the energy between you, can be deeply intimate. Breath is also a form of touch breathing together, syncing your heartbeats, feeling the presence of each other.

Practice: Try placing your forehead against your partners, breathing in sync, feeling your connection without words, without movement, only presence. Honor Touch as a Form of Prayer. If we treat touch as sacred, it becomes a prayer. Let love-making be an act of devotion, a moment of deep reverence, a surrender to love itself.

"My beloved is mine, and I am his." Song of Solomon 2:16

Practice: Before love-making, place your hands on your partner's heart and silently pray for your love, for your connection, and for your souls to merge in sacred unity.

Reflection Questions

Do I touch with presence, or do I rush through moments of connection? How can I use touch as a way to express love, devotion, and comfort?

Do I honor my partner's body as sacred, or do I take it for granted? How can I invite God into my physical connection, making love-making an act of worship?

A Closing Prayer for Sacred Touch.

Lord, let my touch be a reflection of Your love. Let my hands bring comfort, healing, and devotion. May my presence be fully in the moment, honoring the sacredness of love and intimacy. Let my love-making be an offering, a prayer, a divine exchange of energy that reflects Your holy design.
Amen.

NEXT CHAPTER PREVIEW:

The Art of Surrender Letting Go & Receiving Love Fully

In Chapter 9, we will explore:

The power of surrender in love and intimacy. How to release fear and fully receive love.

The divine balance of giving and allowing oneself to be held.

Final Thought:

Love is Spoken Through Touch. Love does not always need words.

Sometimes, it only needs a hand reaching for another, a soft embrace, a presence that says:

I see you. I feel you. I love you.

To touch with reverence is to make love an act of worship, a reflection of divine presence, a language of the soul.

Chapter 9
The Art of Surrender Letting Go & Receiving Love Fully

The Divine Balance Between Giving and Receiving in Love the Sacred Act of Surrender

Love is not just about giving; it is also about receiving.

True intimacy requires both a flow of offering and accepting, of holding and being held, of giving love, and surrendering to love.

Yet, surrendering is often the hardest part.

To surrender means to trust, to let go, to allow yourself to be seen, touched, and cherished without fear.

"Be still and know that I am God." Psalm 46:10

Surrender is not a weakness; it is a strength in its purest form. It is the ability to say:

I trust love more than I fear it.

I allow myself to be held, to be seen, to be fully known. I open my heart not just to give love but to receive it.

In this chapter, we will explore:

The power of surrender in love and intimacy. How to release fear and fully receive love.

The divine balance of giving and allowing oneself to be held. What Does It Mean to Surrender in Love?

Surrender in intimacy is not about losing control. It is about releasing fear. It means Letting go of the need to protect yourself from love.

Allowing your partner to see you, touch you, and love you fully. Trusting that you are safe, cherished, and worthy of love.

Many people give love freely but struggle to receive love deeply. They build walls, fearing that surrender means losing themselves.

But surrender is not about losing yourself. It is about stepping into something greater than yourself.

"There is no fear in love, but perfect love drives out fear." 1 John 4:18

Surrender is where love becomes effortless, where intimacy becomes profound, and where two souls merge in divine unity.

The Fear of Surrendering to Love. Why do so many struggles to fully let go of love-making? Because surrender means Trusting another with your heart, your body, and your soul.

Releasing control, allowing yourself to be vulnerable. Giving up the fear of being hurt, abandoned, or misunderstood. Many holds onto emotional armor, believing: I surrender, I might get hurt. If I open too much, I may be rejected. If I let myself feel too deeply, it might be taken away. But love cannot fully flow where there is fear. Love requires openness, trust, and a willingness to let go.

"Commit your way to the Lord; trust in Him, and He will act." Psalm 37:5

The more you cling to fear, the less you allow love to enter. The more you trust, the deeper intimacy will become. The Balance of Giving and Receiving in Love-Making. Sacred intimacy is a dance between giving and receiving. Giving Love: Offering touch, presence, and devotion. Receiving Love: Allowing yourself to be held, adored, and cherished. Many struggles with receiving, they feel guilty, undeserving, or unworthy of deep love. But to truly experience divine love, you must allow yourself to be fully loved.

"You are altogether beautiful, my love; there is no flaw in you." Song of Solomon 4:7

Surrendering to love is an act of faith. Allowing yourself to be touched, kissed, and held without resistance is an act of trust. Receiving love is just as holy as giving it. When both partners give and receive freely, love-making becomes a sacred exchange, a reflection of divine unity.

How to Surrender in Love & Intimacy to practice surrendering in love, try these sacred steps:

Let Go of Control Release the need to plan, manage, or predict the moment. Let love flow naturally, without force or expectation.

Trust that intimacy is not about performance but presence.

Trust in the Lord with all your heart and lean not on your own understanding." Proverbs 3:5

Practice: Close your eyes and take deep breaths before intimacy. Imagine yourself letting go, allowing love to lead. Be Fully Present, Surrender is about being in the moment fully, completely. Feel every touch, every breath, every heartbeat.

Let go of thoughts, distractions, or worries.

Practice: Before love-making, place your hand on your partner's heart. Breathe together, synchronizing your energy, feeling the connection without words.

Allow Yourself to Be Loved. Instead of giving love constantly, practice receiving it. Allow yourself to be kissed, touched, and adored without resistance.

Accept that you are worthy of deep, unconditional love.

"I have loved you with an everlasting love." Jeremiah 31:3

Practice: The next time your partner touches you, pause. Instead of immediately responding, simply receive it, feel it, and surrender to it.

See Surrender as a Sacred Offering. Surrendering in love is not about giving into it, it's about giving in. It is about trusting the moment, the love, the divine connection.

When you surrender, you offer yourself as an act of devotion.

I am my beloved, and my beloved is mine." Song of Solomon 6:3

Practice: Before love-making, say a silent prayer:

Let me be fully present in love. Let me surrender without fear and receive love as You have designed it.

Reflection Questions:

Do I trust love fully, or do I hold back in fear?

How can I allow myself to receive love more deeply? What fears keep me from surrendering fully to intimacy?

How can I see surrender as an act of divine trust rather than a loss of control?

A Closing Prayer for Surrender

Lord, help me to release fear and fully trust in love. Let me surrender, not in weakness, but in faith. Let me receive love as a divine gift, allowing myself to be held, cherished, and adored as You intended. Let my love-making be a sacred offering, a moment of deep connection, and a reflection of Your divine presence.

Amen.

NEXT CHAPTER PREVIEW:

The Spiritual Covenant of Love Intimacy as a Reflection of God's Eternal Love

In Chapter 10, we will explore:

How love-making mirrors God's covenant of love.

The deeper spiritual significance of unity in relationships. How intimacy can be a pathway to divine transformation.

Final Thought:

Surrender is the Gateway to True Intimacy

To surrender in love is to say:

I trust this love.

I trust this connection.

I trust that I am safe, adored, and worthy of receiving love as deeply as I give it.

When we let go, when we open, when we surrender, we step into the fullness of love as God designed it.

Chapter 10
The Spiritual Covenant of Love and Intimacy as a Reflection of God's Eternal Love

The Art of Understanding Hearing Beyond Words In the sacred bond of love, understanding is more than just hearing words. It is about perceiving the heart behind them. True intimacy is not only physical but also emotional and spiritual. To truly merge as one, couples must learn to communicate beyond language, to hear what is not being said, and to discern the deeper meaning in each other expressions.

How Love-Making Mirrors God's Covenant of Love God designed intimacy to be a reflection of His divine covenant, an eternal, unbreakable bond built on love, trust, and unity. Just as God pursues us with love, offering Himself fully and desiring a deep relationship with us, intimacy in a marriage is meant to be an expression of that same devotion.

Love-making is a sacred act of commitment, a continual renewal of the vow to love, cherish, and honor one another, just as God remains faithful to His people.

It requires sacrifice and selflessness. True intimacy is not about taking; it is about giving. Just as Christ gave Himself for us, love-making is a gift of self, a surrender to love's higher purpose.

It deepens connection and trust Just as our relationship with God grows stronger when we draw near to Him in vulnerability, physical intimacy strengthens the bond between two souls, knitting them together in an unspoken language of love.

When love-making is approached with reverence, it becomes more than a physical experience; it becomes a mirror of God's divine love, an act of worship through which couples can experience the beauty of sacred union.

The Deeper Spiritual Significance of Unity in Relationships The unity between a husband and wife is not just emotional or physical; it is spiritual. God's design for marriage is a reflection of His unity with us, calling couples into an oneness that transcends the earthly.

Becoming one flesh is more than physical connections. It is the merging of souls, hearts, and minds in a way that reflects divine harmony.

Love in its highest form purifies and transforms. When love is rooted in God, it becomes a force of healing, refining each partner to become more like Christ.

Unity in relationships reflects God's wholeness. Just as God is three in one Father, Son, and Spirits, a couple joined in sacred love embodies a completeness that brings divine order and balance.

When couples understand the spiritual weight of their union, they approach intimacy with reverence, seeing it as a divine gift rather than a mere act. Love becomes not just something they share but something that continually shapes and transforms them.

How Intimacy Can Be a Pathway to Divine Transformation Intimacy is more than pleasure; it is a pathway to transformation. When approached with spiritual awareness, love-making becomes a sacred practice that deepens connection, expands love, and draws couples closer to God.

It opens the heart to vulnerability. True intimacy requires removing walls and allowing oneself to be fully seen, just as we must open ourselves to God to experience His presence.

It teaches surrender and trust in sacred love, and we learn to let go, to trust our partner completely, mirroring the way we are called to trust in God's love for us.

It renews and restores. Just as worship refreshes the soul, intimacy, when done in love, renews the bond between two people, healing wounds and strengthening their unity.

When love-making is guided by divine purpose, it ceases to be just an act; it becomes an experience of God's presence, a sacred space where love, energy, and spirit intertwine in a way that brings transformation.

Final Thought:

Surrender is the Gateway to True Intimacy At the heart of divine intimacy is surrender, the willingness to let go of fear, self-protection, and pride in order to fully give and receive love. Just as we must surrender to God to experience His love completely, we must surrender to our beloved to experience the fullness of intimacy.

Surrender is trust, allowing oneself to be held, known, and cherished. Surrender is openness, welcoming love without fear or resistance.

Surrender is divine, reflecting the way Christ gave Himself fully for us.

When love is approached with surrender, intimacy becomes more than an exchange; it becomes a spiritual experience, a moment of divine connection where two souls become one, reflecting the eternal covenant of God's love.

True intimacy is not about control or performance. It is about presence, devotion, and the willingness to fully embrace love as God designed it. It is in surrender that love reaches its highest form, where the soul finds rest, and where the sacred mystery of two becoming one is fully realized.

Chapter 11 The Temple of Love Honoring the Body as Sacred

As the journey through divine intimacy deepens, the next chapter will explore the sacred nature of the body and how honoring it is essential to experiencing love as God intended.

In this chapter, we will explore:

1. The Body as a Temple A Vessel of Divine Love.

Understanding that our bodies are not just flesh but holy vessels created for love and connection.

How treating the body with reverence enhances intimacy and strengthens the bond between partners.

The significance of purity not just in abstinence but in how we care for and honor our bodies as sacred gifts from God.

2. The Connection Between the Physical and the Spiritual

How what we do with our bodies affects the spirit, mind, and emotions.

The energetic exchange of love-making why intimacy is more than physical touch but a spiritual act.

How respecting, nourishing, and cherishing the body elevates the experience of love and union.

3. Healing the Temple Releasing Shame and Embracing Wholeness

Addressing past wounds, traumas, or misconceptions about the body that may hinder true intimacy.

Learning to see oneself and one's partner through Gods eyes as fearfully and wonderfully made.

How love-making can be a healing experience when approached with intentionality, trust, and divine love.

4. Worship Through Love Experiencing the Divine in the Physical.

Seeing intimacy as a sacred act of worship, where love and Gods presence meet.

How sensuality, when guided by love and respect, can bring couples into a deeper connection with the divine.

The mystery of God's presence dwelling within the union of two souls, reflecting His eternal love.

A Sacred Invitation In chapter eleven, we will unveil how treating the body as a sacred temple elevates love-making into a divine experience, one that is free of shame, full of reverence, and deeply connected to Gods design.

Chapter 11
The Temple of Love Honoring the Body as Sacred

As the journey through divine intimacy deepens, this chapter will explore the sacred nature of the body and how honoring it is essential to experiencing love as God intended. When love-making is approached with reverence, it becomes more than an act; it becomes a spiritual practice, a moment where two souls meet in divine unity.

1. The Body as a Temple: A Vessel of Divine Love

Our bodies are not just flesh; they are sacred vessels created for love, connection, and divine expression.

To truly honor intimacy, we must first honor our own bodies and our partners body not as objects of desire but as expressions of God's craftsmanship.

The way we treat, nourish, and prepare our bodies influences the depth of our connection spiritually, emotionally, and physically.

When we see our bodies as sacred, love-making shifts from being an act to a form of worship.

2. The Connection Between the Physical and the Spiritual

Intimacy is not just a physical experience; it is an energetic, emotional, and spiritual exchange.

Every touch, every breath, every shared moment carries meaning beyond the surface.

Love-making is most powerful when approached with intention, presence, and sacred awareness.

The more couples cultivate spiritual alignment in their connection, the more profound their intimacy becomes.

3. Sacred Rituals for Love-Making: Preparing the Body, Mind, and Spirit

Whether it is the first time together or a seasoned relationship, the act of love-making should be preceded by sacred preparation. Intimacy is not just about reaching a destination; it is about cultivating a deep and meaningful experience.

Sacred Ritual #1: Naked Presence

Begin by sitting together naked, not for the purpose of arousal, but simply to be. Know that in this moment, nakedness is the only expectation.

Talk, pray, and hold one another without the pressure to move beyond this space.

This practice fosters trust, vulnerability, and deep emotional connection, allowing each partner to feel fully accepted as they are.

Sacred Ritual #2: The Ritual of Cleansing

Prepare a shared shower or bath as a ritual of purification.

Let water become a symbol of renewal, washing away stress, distractions, and emotional burdens.

Engage in gentle conversation, laughter, or silent appreciation of one another.

Allow intimacy to exist without pressure or expectation, simply as a moment of presence.

This ritual reminds couples that love is not just about intercourse; it is about connection, energy, and the sacred exchange of presence.

Sacred Ritual #3: The Sensory Altar

Create an intentional space for love-making by engaging the senses.

Light candles, anoint each other with scented oils, play soft music let the atmosphere itself become part of the connection.

Focus on small moments of touch and appreciation, allowing passion to build naturally rather than rushing toward it.

The goal is not just to experience pleasure but to create memories that linger beyond the moment.

Through these rituals, intimacy becomes more than a physical act. It becomes sacred, intentional, and deeply spiritual.

4. Healing the Temple Releasing Shame and Embracing Wholeness

Many people carry past wounds, shame, or misconceptions about their bodies and intimacy.

Healing happens in sacred connection when love-making is approached with reverence, safety, and trust.

Seeing the body through God's eyes allows couples to embrace intimacy without guilt, fear, or performance-based expectations.

In divine intimacy, love is not something to be earned or performed. It is a gift to be shared, honored, and cherished.

5. Worship Through Love, experience the Divine in the Physical.

Love-making, when approached with the right heart, is a form of worship, a way to experience God's presence in the union of two souls.

Sensuality, when guided by love and reverence, becomes a pathway to spiritual awakening.

The divine mystery of intimacy lies in the way two become one, mirroring the eternal covenant of God's love.

When intimacy is treated as sacred, it deepens not just the physical connection but the spiritual bond, allowing love to take on its highest and most divine form.

Final Thought:

Let Love Be Sacred; let intimacy be more than an act. It is a divine ritual. Let love-making become something intentional, something designed with honor, presence, and spiritual connection.

When love is approached in this way, it ceases to be a temporary pleasure. It becomes an eternal imprint on the soul.

PREVIEW OF UPCOMING CHAPTER:

Chapter 12 The Breath of Love Sacred Energy Exchange in Intimacy

Love is more than touch; it is energy, rhythm, and breath. In the next chapter, we will explore how breath, movement, and presence shape the depth of intimacy. Just as God breathed life into humanity, breath within love-making is a sacred force guiding passion, deepening connection, and synchronizing two souls into divine harmony. When couples learn to breathe together, move with intention, and channel their energy with awareness, love-making becomes a sacred dance, one that is not just physical but a merging of spirit and life force. This chapter will introduce techniques to harness the power of breath, how to align energy with one's partner, and how to use stillness as a gateway to transcendent, soul-deep intimacy.

Chapter 12
The Breath of Love's Sacred Energy Exchange in Intimacy

Love is more than touch; it is energy, rhythm, and breath. True intimacy transcends the physical; it is a dance of presence, connection, and divine awareness. Just as God breathed life into humanity, breath within love-making is a sacred force guiding passion, deepening connection, and synchronizing two souls into divine harmony.

When couples learn to breathe together, move with intention, and channel their energy with awareness, love-making becomes more than an act. It becomes a sacred merging of spirit and life force. This chapter will explore the power of breathwork, energy alignment, and the ability to connect beyond the physical realm.

1. The Sacred Breath Syncing with the Rhythm of Love.

Breath is the essence of life, the bridge between the body and the spirit.

When lovers synchronize their breathing, they create a unified rhythm that deepens connection and awareness.

Intentional breathing during intimacy enhances presence, slows time, and allows love- making to become an immersive, meditative experience.

Practice: The Breath of Love

1. Sit or lie together, facing each other.

2. Begin breathing slowly, allowing your breath to rise and fall in sync.

3. With each inhale, receive your partner's energy; with each exhale, offer your love and presence.

4. As the breath deepens, let the rhythm guide your movement and connection.

The more in tune a couple becomes with their breath, the more effortless intimacy feels flowing as one, guided by a divine pulse.

2. Energy Alignment Merging Beyond the Physical.

Intimacy is an energetic exchange. Every touch, glance, and breath carry a vibration.

Being fully present with your partner creates an invisible thread of connection that deepens love beyond words or actions.

By tuning into each other's energy, couples learn to feel one another in ways that transcend the physical.

Practice: The Silent Connection

1. Instead of speaking, sit together in silence, eyes locked, breathing in harmony.

2. Feel the energy between you, allowing emotions, love, and intention to pass through without words.

3. Place your hands over each other's heart, sensing the warmth and the unspoken connection.

Over time, this practice builds a deep, energetic bond, allowing couples to communicate without touch, without sound, only presence.

3. Connecting Beyond Distance Strengthening Spiritual Intimacy: Intimacy is not limited by space. Love is energy, and energy knows no bounds. When couples learn to connect spiritually, their bond remains strong even when apart.

Close your eyes and envision your partner's presence beside you. Breathe deeply, feeling their energy as if they were right there.

Send love, warmth, and intention through thought, allowing them to feel your presence wherever they are.

Trust that your souls are always intertwined, regardless of physical distance.

By cultivating spiritual inventiveness, couples strengthen their connection beyond time and space, proving that love is not just physical but a force that transcends reality itself.

4. The Power of Stillness: The Ultimate Sacred Exchange. Love is not only found in movements; it is found in stillness.

Sometimes, the most intimate moments come not from action but from being fully present in silence.

Love-making is not just about passion; it is about dwelling in each other's energy and feeling safe, seen, and whole.

The highest form of intimacy is surrendering to the moment, allowing energy to flow without force, without expectations, only presence.

Practice: The Stillness of Love

1. Lie together, touching lightly or not at all.

2. Close your eyes and breathe, absorbing the essence of your beloved.

3. Feel the space between you; it's energy and power.

4. Let the moment exist without words, without movement, just connection.

The greatest intimacy is not just in what is done but in what is felt.

Final Thought:

Love as a Divine Frequency.

When love is understood as energy, breath, and intention, intimacy takes on a deeper meaning. It becomes a sacred vibration, a divine exchange that exists beyond the physical.

By practicing breathwork, stillness, and energetic connection, whether together or apart, couples discover that true intimacy is never limited by flesh. Instead, it is a sacred force that moves through time, space, and spirit, uniting souls in divine harmony.

Sacred Ritual: The Essence of Oneness Connecting Beyond Space Intimacy is not bound by proximity; true connection transcends distance. When two souls are deeply intertwined, they do not need to see or touch to feel one another presence. This ritual is designed for couples who wish to practice the art of oneness, even in separate spaces, strengthening their bond through memory, scent, and spiritual attunement.

Step 1: The Ritual of Scent Holding the Essence of Your Beloved

Every person carries a unique scent, an invisible fingerprint of the soul. It is more than fragrance. It is memory, energy, and familiarity woven into the subconscious.

1. Choose an item infused with your partner's natural scent, perhaps a shirt, a pillow, a scarf, or something they've worn. If apart, use an oil or fragrance they often wear.

2. Hold the item close; breathe it in deeply. Let the scent awaken your memory, bringing the presence of your beloved into your mind's eye.

3. Close your eyes and allow the scent to take shape as a feeling of warmth, a sense of home, a comfort only they bring.

4. Linger in this space, allowing your body to recognize its essence, knowing it is a bridge to them, even when they are not physically nearby.

When you know and memorize your partner's scent deeply, your brain registers it as a living presence, allowing you to feel them as though they are with you.

Step 2: The Meditation of Presence Finding Each Other in the Unseen

Once you have attuned yourself to your beloved's essence, take the practice deeper, finding one another through energy alone.

1. Find a quiet space separate from your partner, in another room, or in a completely different location. Sit or lie comfortably, closing your eyes.

2. Breathe deeply, slowing your thoughts. Focus on nothing but your partners' presence.

3. Call them into your awareness. Imagine them as if they are sitting in front of you. Feel their warmth, their breath, their energy.

4. Hold the vision with clarity. Picture their expressions, their heartbeat, the way their spirit feels next to yours.

5. Reach for them in the unseen. Imagine touching their face, tracing their hands, embracing them. Let your soul remember the feeling.

The more you practice finding each other in spirit, the stronger your energetic bond becomes. This connection will manifest in your waking life, allowing you to sense your partner before they enter a room, feel their emotions even when they don't speak, and long for them in a way that is beyond the physical.

Step 3: The Memory of the Souls Carrying Each Other Within.

Once you have mastered the ability to recognize your partner's essence through scent, memory, and energy, intimacy reaches a new depth, one where longing is not about absence but about deep awareness of each other's being.

The next time you are physically together, pay attention to how your body responds before they arrive. Do you sense them approaching? Does your heartbeat change? Close your eyes when near them and breathe them in. Let your sensory memory take over, recognizing their presence without sight.

Deepen this ritual by becoming familiar with their heartbeat, their warmth, their rhythms; these are all part of their soul's signature, just like their scent.

When two souls learn to recognize each other beyond sight, beyond touch, beyond words, they create an intimacy that cannot be broken by time, space, or circumstance.

This is the art of becoming one, even in separation.

For this sacred ritual of love-making and deep, energetic connection, essential oils play a powerful role in enhancing intimacy, memory, and spiritual attunement. The right oils awaken the senses, heighten the emotional connection, and imprint the essence of your beloved into your mind, creating a lasting sensory bond.

Here are some of the best essential oils to use for this ritual:

1. Rose in The Oil of Divine Love

Symbolizes unconditional love, passion, and devotion. Awakens the heart chakra, deepening emotional connection. Enhances feelings of intimacy, trust, and tenderness.

Perfect for: Anointing the body, adding to a bath, or using in a diffuser during love-making.

How to Use: Apply a few drops on your pulse points (wrists, neck, and heart) before the ritual to carry your partners' essence with you.

2. Sandalwood The Oil of Sacred Union

Grounds the body and spirit, aligning energies for deeper intimacy.

Known for its warm, sensual aroma that heightens attraction and connection.

Encourages presence, slowing down the mind to focus on the now.

Perfect for Massage, diffusing in the bedroom, or placing a drop on the chest before meditation.

How to Use: Add a few drops to a carrier oil for a slow, intentional massage before love- making, creating a deep energetic bond.

3. Jasmine The Oil of Sensual Awakening

Enhances desire, confidence, and the flow of energy between lovers.

Known as a natural aphrodisiac, increasing physical and emotional attraction. Helps release inhibitions, allowing deeper surrender into intimacy.

Perfect for Rubbing onto the lower abdomen, diffusing during love-making, or anointing a pillow with its scent.

How to Use: Place a drop on your hands, rub together, and inhale before engaging in deep breathing with your partner to sync your energy.

4. Ylang Ylang The Oil of Passion & Playfulness
Stimulates sensuality, arousal, and deep relaxation. Encourages emotional openness and vulnerability.

Balances male and female energies, fostering harmony in love-making.

Perfect for Diluting with a carrier oil and using for anointing or placing in a bath before intimacy.

How to Use: Add a few drops to a warm bath and soak together, allowing the aroma to create a sacred atmosphere for love-making.

5. Frankincense: The Oil of Divine Connection

Elevates intimacy from physical to spiritual, creating a sacred experience. Deepens meditation, prayer, and energetic merging.

Helps both partners become fully present, enhancing touch and emotional connection.

Perfect for: Anointing each other before love-making, prayer rituals, or breathwork exercises.

How to Use: Place a drop on each partners forehead before beginning the ritual to invite divine energy into the union.

6. Vetiver The Oil of Grounded Passion

Anchors energy, slowing things down to deepen presence and awareness. Creates a sense of safety, stability, and deep masculine-feminine connection. Enhances touch, making sensations richer and more meaningful.

Perfect for Rubbing onto the soles of the feet, diffusing in the bedroom, or massaging into the lower back.

How to Use: Warm a few drops in your palms and massage your partners shoulders and back, helping them release tension and fully surrender to the moment.

7. Neroli: The Oil of Emotional Intimacy

Encourages deep emotional connection and vulnerability.

Helps release past wounds or insecurities, opening the heart to deeper love. Softens energy, bringing a sense of peace and trust between partners.

Perfect for: Anointing before spiritual connection practices, placing on pulse points, or diffusing while meditating together.

When lovers memorize each other's scent, whether natural or enhanced by sacred oils, it becomes a fingerprint of the soul. The more familiar you become with it, the more your body and spirit recognize your beloved even in their absence.

Through intentional use of scent, breath, and energy, intimacy transforms into something eternal, something sacred, an experience that lingers long after the moment has passed.

Chapter 13
Protecting the Sacred Union Guarding Love from Outside Influence

Love, in its truest form, is sacred. When two souls come together in divine intimacy, their union becomes a living sanctuary, a space where trust, vulnerability, and deep connection flourish. Yet, even the strongest love can be tested when outside influences creep in.

Whether through societal pressures, family expectations, past wounds, or distractions of the world, external forces can erode the foundation of intimacy if not intentionally guarded.

In this chapter, we will explore how to protect your sacred relationship from external interference, keeping love pure, strong, and deeply aligned with Gods design.

1. Recognizing the Sacredness of Your Union

Before guarding against outside influences, a couple must first understand the sanctity of their bond. Your love is not just an emotional or physical connection. It is a covenant, a spiritual merging designed by God.

Love is a divine space, not a public forum. Not everything in your relationship needs to be shared with friends, family, or social media.

Sacred intimacy is exclusive. It belongs to only two souls, and letting too many voices in can dilute its purity.

"What God joins together, let no one separate" (Mark 10:9)

This means actively protecting love from anything that seeks to divide or weaken it.

When love is treated as a holy sanctuary, outside influences hold less power over it.

2. The Power of Spiritual Boundaries. Keeping the World Out

Boundaries are not about isolation but about preserving the strength of your union. A sacred relationship requires discernment, knowing which influences nurture your love and which ones threaten to weaken it.

Set Emotional & Social Boundaries: Not every concern about your relationship needs outside input. Be selective about who speaks into your love life.

Limit Comparison: The world glorifies relationships built on image, performance, and fleeting passion. True intimacy is not meant to be compared or measured against unrealistic standards.

Guard Your Energy: Protect your time, space, and emotional reserves from unnecessary stressors that could distract or divide.

Filter Advice Through Spirit: Even well-meaning family or friends may not understand the sacred nature of your connection. Always filter guidance through prayer and intuition.

When boundaries of wisdom protect love, it thrives in peace and security.

3. Releasing the Past and Healing Old Influences

Sometimes, the biggest outside influence comes from within past wounds, traumas, and old relationship patterns. If unhealed, these things can seep into intimacy, causing doubt, fear, or insecurity. Break Free from Past Relationships: Emotional ties to past lovers or unhealthy attachments must be fully released to honor the sacredness of your current love.

Heal Family Wounds: If family dynamics have shaped your view of love in unhealthy ways, recognize them and seek healing.

Let Go of Societal Expectations: The world's version of love is often transactional. God's version is eternal, selfless, and deeply spiritual.

Forgive and Renew: Holding onto resentment from past hurts creates walls in intimacy. True love requires constant renewal and grace.

By releasing past interference, you allow your love to grow in purity and strength.

4. The Art of Inner Stillness and Returning to Each Other.

When the world gets loud, love must remain still. One of the most powerful ways to protect intimacy is through intentional stillness moments where nothing exists but each other.

Sacred Practice: The Reset Ritual Whenever you feel the world creeping into your love through stress, conflict, or outside opinions, pause and reset your connection.

1. Sit together in silence. No words, no distractions, just presence.

2. Breathe in sync. Align your energy, remembering that your love is a sacred space.

3. Hold hands or place a hand over each other's heart. Feel the rhythm of your bond.

4. Speak a simple affirmation: This love is ours, this love is sacred, and nothing outside of us holds power over it.

5. Pray together. Ask for God's guidance in keeping your relationship strong against any interference.

By practicing intentional stillness, couples cultivate unbreakable bonds rooted in presence, trust, and divine energy.

5. Strength in Unity Becoming an Unshakable Force

The world may challenge love, but a couple united in spirit cannot be broken.

Prioritize Us Over Everything Else: Let your love be the first priority, not external expectations or obligations.

Move as One: Make decisions together, ensuring that both hearts are fully aligned.

Remain Loyal to the Sacred Bond: Infidelity is not just physical; it can be emotional, mental, or energetic. Keep your love pure, devoted, and exclusive.

Pray & Grow Together: A couple that prays together and builds intimacy with God at the center will withstand any outside storm.

Love that is built on spiritual unity does not crumble under pressure. It only grows stronger.

Final thought:

Guard Your Love as a Divine Sanctuary.

Your love is a sacred covenant, a temple built by God. Not everyone will understand it, and not everyone deserves access to it. But when you protect it with intention, guard it from outside interference, release past burdens, and cultivate inner stillness, it becomes an unshakable force, an eternal sanctuary of love and trust.

The Love Sanctuary Rituals: A Sacred Shield Against Outside Energy

This Prevention Ritual is designed to fortify love before outside influences can take hold, creating a shield around your sacred union. It is for couples who want to be proactive in keeping their relationship free from negative energy, distractions, and external pressures.

This practice helps establish a spiritual force field, ensuring that your love remains pure, unshaken, and deeply aligned with God's intention.

Step 1: Establish the Sanctuary of Love

1. Choose a sacred space where you will perform this ritual in your bedroom, a special part of your home, or any place where you feel deeply connected.

2. Remove all distractions. No phones, no outside noise, no interruptions.

3. Light a candle together, symbolizing the divine presence in your union and the light that keeps darkness away.

4. Anoint each other with protective oils and use frankincense for spiritual protection, myrrh for purification, and sandalwood for grounding.

As you prepare, let the space become a sanctuary, a sacred realm where only love exists. Step 2: The Sacred Declaration of Protection

This is the moment where you and your partner consciously claim your love as sacred and affirm that nothing outside of you will be given power over your union.

hold hands, close your eyes, and speak these words together:

This love is a sanctuary, a temple built by God. We declare that no outside force, opinion, distraction, or interference will enter the sacred space of our love. What is between us is divine, unbreakable, and protected. Only truth, only love, and only unity reside here. We guard this bond with wisdom, trust, and the strength of God's presence. Our love is sacred, our connection eternal, and our hearts are sealed as one.

Amen.

After speaking these words, sit in silence, feeling the presence of divine protection settle over your relationship.

Step 3: The Circle of Light, A Visualization for Protection.

To energetically seal your relationship from outside influence, perform this visualization together:

1. Close your eyes and picture a golden light surrounding both of you.

2. See this light growing stronger, forming an impenetrable circle around your love.

3. Visualize any external distractions, opinions, stress, negativity bouncing off this protective shield, unable to enter.

4. As you breathe in, absorb the love and peace within your sacred space.

5. As you breathe out, release anything that does not belong in your union.

Let this visualization serve as a spiritual boundary, a shield that remains around your relationship beyond the ritual.

Step 4: The Token of Protection

To maintain the strength of this ritual in daily life, choose a physical symbol of protection that reminds you both of your love's sacredness.

This could be:

A small stone or crystal blessed in prayer.

A piece of fabric or cloth anointed with sacred oil.

A piece of jewelry you both wear as a reminder of your commitment.

Each time you feel outside energy trying to enter your love, hold this token, breathe, and recall the protection of your sacred union.

Step 5: Sealing the Ritual in Love.

To close the ritual, hold each other in silence, no words, just presence.

Feel the warmth, the heartbeat, the breath that belongs only to this sacred bond. Let love be the final seal and the strongest protection against all interference.

Optional: If you wish, seal the ritual with a kiss, an embrace, or love-making, whatever feels right to solidify your sacred energy.

How to Use This Ritual Regularly

Perform it once a month to keep your relationship strong and free from interference.

When you sense negative outside energy creeping in, take a moment to repeat the Sacred Declaration of Protection together.

Keep your token of protection near you in your pocket, on your altar, or on your person to remind you of the shield that surrounds your love.

If you ever feel disconnected or distracted, return to this space of stillness and remind yourselves that your love is a sanctuary, untouchable by the outside world.

Final Thought:

A Love That Cannot Be Touched.

A sacred relationship is like a flame, it must be protected from the winds of the world. Not everyone will understand your love. Not everyone needs access to it. By intentionally guarding it, nurturing it, and reaffirming its sanctity, you create a love that remains untouchable, unshaken, and divinely blessed.

Chapter 14
Finding Grace Loving Through Imperfection.

Love, no matter how sacred, is not immune to moments of struggle. Two souls merging into one will inevitably face challenges, misunderstandings, and moments of weakness. True intimacy is not about perfection. It is about grace.

To love deeply is to offer grace freely to hold space for growth, to forgive, to see beyond flaws, and to recognize that love is a journey, not a destination. Grace is the bridge between our humanity and divinity it is what allows love to endure.

In this chapter, we will explore how grace transforms love, how to offer it to one another, and how to receive it as a gift of divine intimacy.

1. The Grace to See Your Partner as God Sees Them.

Love deepens when we learn to see our partner not just through our expectations but through God's eyes.

Every soul carries wounds, past experiences, and struggles that shape how they love.

True intimacy requires compassion an ability to see beyond surface flaws and understand the heart beneath.

Just as God sees us with mercy and unconditional love, we are called to do the same for our beloved.

Sacred Practice: The Mirror of Grace

The next time your partner does something that frustrates or hurts you:

1. Pause before reacting. Breathe, soften, and ask yourself: Am I seeing them with grace or judgment?

2. Reflect on their heart rather than their action. Could this be coming from stress, exhaustion, or an unspoken burden?

3. Offer a silent prayer for clarity: God, help me see them as You see them.

4. Choose love before correction. Instead of responding in frustration, respond with curiosity and care.

Grace is the ability to love beyond what is seen, recognizing that we are all growing, healing, and learning.

2. The Grace of Forgiveness Healing Love Through Compassion.

Forgiveness is one of the highest forms of grace. Love cannot thrive when held hostage by past hurts, resentment, or unspoken wounds.

Holding onto grudges blocks intimacy and it creates walls that separate hearts. Forgiveness does not mean forgetting but choosing love over bitterness.

Just as God extends grace to us endlessly, we must extend it to the one we love.

Sacred Practice: The Forgiveness Ritual

If there is tension, unspoken hurt, or past wounds affecting your love, create a moment of sacred release:

1. Sit facing each other, holding hands.

2. Take a deep breath and close your eyes. Let go of the need to be right, to justify, or to defend.

3. One partner begins by saying: release you from any hurt that has come between us. I choose love over resentment. I choose grace over distance. I forgive, and I invite healing.

4. The other partner responds with the same words.

5. Seal the moment with an embrace, a kiss, or simply resting in silence together.

Forgiveness is not a one-time act. It is a daily commitment to love beyond imperfections.

3. The Grace to Grow Allowing Space for Transformation

No one enters love fully formed. Love itself is a teacher, a refiner, a mirror of growth. Grace means allowing your partner to evolve without demanding immediate perfection. Love is not about fixing each other, but supporting each other journey.

True intimacy means celebrating progress rather than focusing on flaws.

Sacred Practice: The Growth Covenant Instead of seeing struggles as obstacles, view them as opportunities for deepening love.

1. Write down what you admire about your partners growth. What qualities have deepened since you first met? How have they evolved?

2. Share these reflections with each other, acknowledging the beauty of transformation.

3. Set intentions together: What areas do we want to grow in? How can we support each other with grace?

4. Pray over each other's journey, asking for divine guidance in becoming the highest version of yourselves.

Grace creates a space where love can breathe, evolve, and expand without fear of judgment.

4. The Grace to Receive Allowing Love to Hold You. Grace is not just something we give; it is something we must learn to receive.

Many struggles with accepting love when they feel flawed, broken, or undeserving.

True intimacy requires vulnerability the willingness to be loved even in weakness.

Love flourishes when both partners feel safe enough to be imperfect without fear of rejection.

Sacred Practice: The Open Hands Ritual

1. Sit across from your partner, palms facing up.

2. Take turns expressing what you struggle to receive in love. sometimes struggle to let you support me when I feel weak. find it hard to believe I am enough when I make mistakes.

3. As each person speaks, the other gently places their hands over theirs, silently affirming: You are worthy of love. You are enough. I see you, and I will love you through it all.

4. Let the moment sink in and let grace be felt, not just spoken.

Grace allows love to exist in all seasons not just when it is easy, but when it is raw, real, and fully surrendered.

Final Thought:

Grace is the Language of Eternal Love

The most sacred relationships are not built on perfection but on grace. Love that endures is love that learns to:

See beyond flaws and into the heart. Forgive freely and without conditions. Create space for growth without judgment.

Receive love without fear of being unworthy.

Grace is the divine force that keeps love alive not just in moments of passion, but in the quiet, imperfect, and deeply human moments where love is truly tested.

When grace is present, love is unbreakable. This is the love that lasts.

Grace is an active practice one that requires intention, presence, and a willingness to surrender ego for the sake of deeper connection. Below are additional rituals to help couples cultivate grace in their relationship. These practices are designed to foster forgiveness, patience, understanding, and a love that endures through imperfection.

1. The Altar of Grace a Sacred Ritual for Letting Go of Judgments

Sometimes, love is tested not by major conflicts, but by small, accumulating frustrations. This ritual helps couples release unspoken disappointments and refocus on love.

How to Perform the Altar of Grace Ritual:

1. Create a physical or symbolic altar. This could be a small table, a candle, or simply a shared sacred space where you both feel at peace.

2. Write down any judgments, expectations, or frustrations that have been lingering things unsaid but felt.

3. Read your notes aloud, not as accusations but as reflections. For example:

I have felt frustrated when I don't feel heard, but I realize this comes from my own need to control how I listen.

I have held resentment when you withdraw, but I now recognize that you process emotions differently than I do.

4. After sharing, place the notes in a bowl and burn them (safely) or tear them up.

Speak this affirmation together: release all judgments. I choose to see you through love, not expectation. I accept you fully, as you are.

5. Close with a moment of physical connection and hold hands, embracing, or resting in silence together.

By practicing the release of expectations, couples create space for grace to fill the relationship with patience, understanding, and unconditional love.

2. The Grace Walk Learning to See Your Partner anew.

When grace is missing in love, partners begin to see only what is wrong rather than all that is beautiful. This practice resets the way you perceive each other.

How to Perform the Grace Walk Ritual:

1. Set aside a day where you focus solely on observing your partner through the lens of grace.

2. Notice their small acts of love and the way they look at you, the way they move, the effort they make, the kindness in their tone.

3. At the end of the day, sit together and share:

Today, I noticed you did [this] for me, and I felt deeply loved.

I saw the way you [handled this situation], and I admire your strength. I realized today how much I appreciate [this about you].

4. Let the conversation flow naturally into gratitude and appreciation.

By actively seeing each other anew, couples shift from frustration to admiration, allowing grace to become the foundation of love.

3. The Grace Embrace Holding Each Other in Unspoken Forgiveness

Words don't always heal wounds sometimes; the heart simply needs to feel love rather than hear it. This ritual is about offering grace through presence and touch rather than conversation.

How to Perform the Grace Embrace Ritual:

1. When tension arises, or if you feel disconnected, pause before reacting.

2. Without speaking, approach your partner and open your arms in an invitation for an embrace.

3. Hold each other in complete silence for at least two minutes. Feel their breath, their heartbeat, the warmth of their presence.

4. Let the embrace serve as an unspoken I love you. I choose grace. I choose us.

5. If words feel necessary after, let them come naturally but often, this simple act of physical surrender is enough to dissolve tension and restore intimacy.

Grace is often found not in explanations, but in presence in simply choosing to be there for one another.

4. The Prayer of Grace a Divine Renewal for Love Grace flows most freely when couples invite God into their relationship. This prayer ritual is a moment of surrender, asking for divine wisdom, patience, and unconditional love to fill the partnership.

How to Perform the Prayer of Grace Ritual:

1. Sit together, holding hands or placing a hand over each other's heart.

2. Close your eyes and take a deep breath, releasing tension.

3. Speak this prayer aloud (or in your own words):

God, we come before You as two imperfect souls, learning to love as You have loved us. We ask for Your grace to fill our hearts to soften our words, to ease our judgments, to remind us that love is not about perfection, but about patience, forgiveness, and understanding. Teach us to extend the same grace to one another that You extend to us daily. Let our love be a reflection of Your divine love is steadfast, unconditional, and eternal.

Amen.

4. Sit in silence for a moment, allowing the energy of grace to settle between you.

Couples who pray together create a love that is spiritually fortified, capable of withstanding trials and growing through every challenge.

5. The Grace Letter a Written Act of Love Beyond Mistakes Words hold power. When spoken in frustration, they can cause wounds. When written in love, they can heal. This ritual allows couples to express grace through the written word, offering a letter of love beyond mistakes.

How to Perform the Grace Letter Ritual:

1. Each partner writes a letter that begins with:

I choose grace because

I love you not just for who you are, but for who we are becoming together, even when we struggle, I am grateful for you.

2. Exchange letters and read them privately.

3. Afterward, sit together and hold hands, letting the words sink in before speaking.

4. If desired, share a few thoughts aloud what moved you, what made you feel seen, what you want to strengthen.

Grace is not just about forgiveness it is about choosing to love fully, despite imperfection.

Final Thought:

Grace is the Anchor of Lasting Love cannot thrive without grace. It is grace that allows love to: Survive misunderstandings.

Forgive unintentional hurts. See past flaws and into the soul. Grow through every challenge, rather than being broken by them.

A relationship grounded in grace is a relationship that is unbreakable not because it is perfect, but because it is committed to choosing love, every single day.

When two souls meet in grace, love is no longer just an emotion it becomes a sacred devotion, a divine covenant, a mirror of Gods eternal love.

Chapter 15
The Harmony of Love Balancing Passion, Peace, and Presence

Love is a dance between fire and stillness, passion and peace, excitement and deep-rooted comfort. In sacred intimacy, finding balance is essential too much intensity can burn, while too much complacency can cool the connection. A truly harmonious love embraces both passion and peace, knowing when to surrender to desire and when to rest in presence.

In this chapter, we will explore how to cultivate a love that is both deeply passionate and profoundly peaceful, ensuring that intimacy remains sacred, alive, and evolving.

1. The Dual Nature of Love Embracing Fire and Stillness
   Love thrives in both wild intensity and quiet tenderness.

Passion is the sacred spark, the energy that fuels attraction, desire, and connection. It is the fire that keeps love-making alive.

Peace is the sacred stillness, the deep security and trust that allows love to breathe, settle, and remain unshaken.

A relationship that is all passion without peace can become chaotic and unstable. A relationship that is all peace without passion can become dull and disconnected. A sacred union honors both, allowing each to rise and fall in rhythm.

Sacred Practice: The Breath of Balance

1. Sit together and hold hands, breathing in sync.

2. As you inhale, imagine drawing in the fire of passion energy, desire, movement.

3. As you exhale, imagine sinking into the peace of love safety, stillness, deep trust.

4. Let this rhythm guide your love-making and your daily interactions, knowing when to ignite passion and when to rest in presence.

2. The Role of Presence Keeping Love Alive Beyond Desire

Passion is often fueled by newness, but presence is what makes love last.

When couples lose presence in their relationship, passion fades not because love disappears, but because attention weakens.

When you are with your partner, be fully there.

See them, touch them, listen to them as though it is the first time.

Recognize that true intimacy is not just in love-making, but in the way you connect in everyday moments.

Sacred Practice: The 5-Second Rule

1. Each day, pause for 5 seconds before speaking, touching, or responding to your partner.

2. In that pause, become fully present see them, feel them, notice the moment.

3. When passion feels distant, return to presence. It is the doorway back to love.

4. The Ritual of Sacred Passion Lighting the Fire with Intention.

Passion should never be left to chance, it must be nurtured, cultivated, and intentionally rekindled.

Sacred Practice: The Fire Ritual

1. Create a space of passion light candles, play music, use oils that awaken the senses.

2. Exchange a single touch without speaking, letting energy build.

3. Move slowly, letting desire awaken without rushing.

4. Speak a whispered affirmation to each other, such as:

I desire you deeply, body and soul. And you are my fire, my love, my sacred home.

5. Let love-making become an intentional act of worship, allowing passion to flow naturally.

Passion is not about performance, it is about presence, energy, and the sacred exchange of love.

4. The Ritual of Sacred Stillness. Finding Peace in Love

Just as passion must be nurtured, so must peace. In a world full of distractions, peace is an intentional choice.

Sacred Practice: The Stillness Ritual

1. Sit or lie together in silence, touching gently but without expectation.

2. Breathe as one, allowing the moment to unfold naturally.

3. Let your energy merge without words or movement, simply resting in the comfort of one another.

4. Recognize that love is not just in passion, but in the quiet spaces between.

This ritual strengthens emotional and spiritual intimacy, allowing love to exist beyond physical desire.

5. The Divine Rhythm of Love, Honoring the Cycles of Intimacy.

Love is not static, it moves in waves, cycles, and seasons.

Some moments are filled with intense passion, longing, and desire.

Some moments are meant for rest, stillness, and deep emotional bonding. Neither phase is better or worse, both are essential to divine union.

When couples understand that love has seasons, they stop chasing passion and start honoring the flow.

Sacred Practice: The Love Reflection

1. Reflect on your current season of love. Are you in a phase of fire or a phase of stillness?

2. Honor where you are, rather than forcing a different energy.

3. Ask each other: What do you need more of right now passion or peace? How can we nurture what we are experiencing rather than resist it?

By embracing the rhythm of love, couples find harmony instead of forcing connection. Final Thought: Love is a Sacred Dance of Fire and Stillness

True love is never just passion or just peace, it is the balance of both.

Passion brings energy, excitement, and depth. Peace brings security, trust, and grounding. When held together in harmony, they create a love that is eternal, sacred, and whole.

When couples learn to flow between passion and presence, their love-making becomes a divine exchange one that is endlessly alive, deeply fulfilling, and always sacred.

The Dance of Love Movement as a Sacred Connection

Dance is the perfect embodiment of both fire and stillness, existing between passion and peace. In love, movement is more than physical it is an unspoken language, a rhythm of connection, a way to express intimacy beyond words.

In the fire stage, dance is raw, wild, and untamed a celebration of passion, energy, and desire.

In the still stage, dance is slow, intimate, and grounding, a way to hold warmth without needing to ignite the flames.

A slow dance in stillness is not about seduction but about presence, trust, and shared energy. It is the space where two souls simply exist together no pressure, no urgency, just the comfort of knowing that love is alive in the smallest of moments.

The Sacred Practice of Slow Dancing in Stillness

This ritual is about learning to move together in peace, holding sensuality as a space of joy, rather than just desire.

How to Perform the Still Dance Ritual:

1. Play soft, slow music not to create passion, but to create warmth.

2. Stand close, holding each other with no rush, no agenda.

3. Move gently, swaying, feeling the natural rhythm of each other's bodies.

4. Breathe in sync, allowing stillness to be the only intention.

5. Let hands trace slowly, let foreheads touch learning the joy of simply being close.

6. Close your eyes and just feel the moment.

In this dance, nakedness does not need to lead to passion it can lead to comfort, familiarity, and deep safety.

Being sensual is not just about arousal it is about happiness, playfulness, and feeling truly present in one another's space. Sensuality is the warmth between passion and peace, a place that can ignite desire, but does not have to.

Why This Matters in Sacred Intimacy Couples often associate physical closeness with the expectation of sex. But learning to be naked together, to hold each other without pressure, allows love to breathe.

Dancing is a way to stay connected, even in moments of stillness.

Sensuality is the bridge between stillness and passion, a place where intimacy remains alive, without force or expectation.

By embracing slow, intentional movement, couples keep the warmth alive not just through desire, but through deep, peaceful connection.

Final Thought:

The Dance of Love is Eternal Passion may rise and fall, but the ability to move together, to hold warmth, and to simply exist in sensual presence is what keeps love alive.

So, dance is not just in the fire, but in the stillness. Let love be the music, let trust be the rhythm, and let your connection be the dance that never ends.

Chapter 16
The Song of Love: Let Music Fill Your Essence

Music has a way of awakening the soul, igniting emotions, and deepening connection beyond words. A single song can transport you, shift your energy, and draw you into the essence of love. Just as breath and touch are sacred in intimacy, so too are the words and melodies that weave into the soul.

When lovers share music, they share more than sound they share a piece of themselves. A song can become a portal to memory, passion, comfort, and transcendence. Whether it's the haunting sensuality of Sade, the deep ache of longing, or the bliss of devotion, the right song doesn't' t just play, it fills you.

This chapter explores how music can be used as a pathway to sacred intimacy as a way to feel each other, hold each other, and merge through sound.

1. The Power of Music in Love When a Song Becomes a Shared Essence

Some songs are more than melodies; they become imprints of a moment, a feeling, a connection.

A song can transport you back to the first time you touched, the first time you locked eyes, the first-time love felt eternal.

A song can fill the space between words, saying things that the heart feels but cannot speak.

A song can bring two people into complete energetic harmony, syncing their emotions, breath, and presence.

Some songs awaken passion, others bring comfort, and some make lovers fall into each other's arms as though no time has passed.

What is your song? What melody makes you feel your partner's essence, even when they are not there?

2. The Ritual of the Shared Song, A Practice in Deep Presence

This ritual is designed to let music become an energy exchange between lovers to use a song not just to listen but to feel, absorb, and merge with one another's essence.

How to Perform the Shared Song Ritual:

1. Choose a song that speaks to your connection. It can be sensual, spiritual, nostalgic, or deeply personal.

2. Sit or lie together in silence, facing each other or holding hands.

3. Play the song and close your eyes. Let the music wash over you, breathe into you, fill the space between you.

4. Sync your breath with the rhythm. If the song is slow, let your breathing slow. If it is deep and passionate, feel your body respond.

5. Feel your partner's essence within the music. Imagine their energy flowing into you through the melody.

6. When the song ends, remain in silence, letting the energy linger.

7. If you feel moved, whisper what you felt, what the song awakened, or simply hold each other, letting the moment speak for itself.

This ritual teaches couples to experience intimacy through sound, rather than touch alone.

3. When Music Becomes Memory: The Imprint of a Song

There are certain songs that, when played, bring back the scent, the warmth, the energy of a person.

The song that played during your first kiss.

The song that carried you through heartache and reunion. The song that makes love-making feel like worship.

A song shared in intimacy never leaves you. It becomes woven into your soul, imprinted in your body.

Imagine this: You are apart from your lover. You press play on a song. Instantly, you feel them. Their presence fills you, even from miles away.

That is the power of sound. That is the sacred energy of music.

4. The Practice of Sound and Touch while Merging Music with Sensuality

Music is not just for the ears; it is for the body, the soul, the skin. When you bring music into touch, intimacy becomes a living symphony.

Sacred Practice: The Sound and Touch Connection

1. Choose a song that moves you both, one that carries energy, sensuality, or deep emotion.

2. One partner closes their eyes while the other slowly moves their hands over their skin, syncing touch with the rhythm.

3. Let your hands follow the sound where does the music lead you? Is it slow and intentional? Does it call for deep, lingering connection?

4. Switch roles, let the other person receive.

5. When the song ends, hold each other, letting the music' s energy linger between you.

This practice turns a song into an extension of intimacy, making the body and music one.

5. The Music of Breath, Creating Your Own Song

Even without instruments, without lyrics, love itself is a song. The sound of breathing together in unison.

The quiet hum of contentment in an embrace.

The whispered words that only two souls can understand.

Every love story has a melody, a rhythm, and a heartbeat. Sometimes, the most powerful music is not played; it is felt, breathed, and lived.

Sacred Practice: The Unheard Song

1. Turn off all music. Sit together in silence.

2. Listen to each other's breathing, the subtle shifts of movement, and the sound of presence itself.

3. Lean in, let foreheads touch, and hum softly together, creating your song, your own shared vibration.

4. Let this be a reminder that even without sound, love has music of its own. Final Thought: Let Music Carry Your Love Beyond Time

Some lovers leave an imprint on your soul, just like a song that never fades.

Let music be more than background noise; let it be a portal, a connection, and a way to feel each other's presence even in silence.

When a song fills your essence, it is no longer just music. It is a love that exists beyond words, beyond touch, and beyond time itself.

This practice works great when working on your soulful self. Let the words of a song fill your essence with that song. Sade fills every part of me with her words. I find something so profound that I feel the essence of each word of "By Your Side" in that song.

Music has the power to ignite intimacy and bring you closer, even when you're apart. A song becomes a channel for the connection, something that resonates beyond the physical, reaching the soul's deepest parts.

The Frequency of Love Nurturing the Essence of Your Connection Music is more than sounds; it is frequency, vibration, and energy. When two souls connect through a song, they are not just hearing the same melody; they are tuning into the same frequency, aligning their hearts to a shared rhythm.

Developing a shared frequency in love means creating something that is uniquely you're something that holds your essence, something that lingers even in silence.

A song. A scent.

A phrase whispered in the dark.

A rhythm in the way you hold each other.

When love has a frequency, it is never truly absent. Even in distance, even in quiet moments, you can tune into it, feel it, remember it.

Nurture that essence. Protect it. Feed it. Keep it alive by returning to the things that remind you of who you are together.

Listen to the songs that bring you back to each other. Speak the words that keep your energy connected.

Hold space for stillness, where presence alone is enough.

When love is nurtured, its frequency never fades, it only deepens, becoming something timeless, something eternal.

Chapter 17
The Language of Devotional Words, Affirmations, and Prayers in Sacred Love

Love is not only felt, it is spoken, breathed, and declared. The words we choose in love have power. They can ignite passion, build trust, nurture intimacy, and create a deep spiritual connection between two souls.

Just as love has a frequency, it also has a language, a rhythm of words, and affirmations that shape the essence of your relationship. Whether whispered in the quiet of the night, spoken in the heat of passion, or prayed in moments of stillness, words hold the ability to transform love into something eternal.

This chapter explores the sacred language of love, including how to speak life into your relationship, how to use affirmations to deepen intimacy, and how prayer becomes the foundation of a divine union.

1. The Power of Words in Love: What You Speak, You Create Love is not just an emotion; it is a living energy that is strengthened or weakened by the words spoken between lovers.

Words can heal or harms they can create trust or build walls. Words can ignite passion in the right phrase, and whisperers can awaken desire instantly.

Words can anchor love through time repeated affirmations become the foundation of intimacy.

Reflection: What Words Define Your Love?

What is the most beautiful thing your partner has ever said to you? What words make you feel safe, desired, seen?

What phrases do you return to, again and again, to remind you of your connection?

Words shape the way we see, feel, and experience love they are a sacred gift, meant to be used with intention.

2. The Ritual of Spoken Devotion Affirming Love Daily

Speaking daily words of devotion is a practice that keeps love alive and present, ensuring that connection is never taken for granted.

Sacred Practice: The Devotion Affirmation

Each morning or night, take turns speaking words of devotion to one another.

1. Face each other, hold hands, and breathe deeply.

Speak affirmations that reaffirm love and presence: choose you today, as I did yesterday, and as I will tomorrow. You are safe with me, always.

Your soul is known, your heart is cherished, your love is my home.

2. Let your partner receive the words fully, without response it's just feeling them.

3. After both have spoken, embrace, sealing the words with presence.

By making spoken devotion a daily ritual, love is continuously affirmed and reinforced, keeping connection strong through every season.

3. The Power of Whispered Words in Intimacy

Words are not just for everyday love; they are tools of deep sensuality and passion.

A single phrase, spoken at the right moment, can: Heighten desire. Deepen connection. Anchor a lover fully into the present moment. Sensual Words to Use in Intimacy I feel you. You are mine, and I am yours. Stay here, right here, with me.

Your touch is home. You are more than my desire; you are my devotion.

Practice: The Whispered Word Ritual

1. During love-making, pause and speak a phrase softly into your partner ear.

2. Let the words be slow, intentional each one carrying weight.

3. Feel how words change the energy between you, making presence deeper, connection stronger.

Passion is not just about movement; it is about the language you create within intimacy.

4. The Sacred Power of Prayer in Love

Love, at its highest level, is a divine covenant a reflection of God's eternal love. Speaking prayers over your relationship is a way to protect, strengthen, and align your love with something greater than yourselves.

The Union Prayer Ritual

1. Sit together, hold hands, and close your eyes.

2. One partner begins God, we invite You into our love. Bless this union, protect this connection, and keep our hearts aligned with You.

3. The other partner follows: Lord, our words be gentle, our love be pure, and our devotion be steadfast. Let our connection be sacred, unbreakable, and always rooted in truth.

4. Seal the prayer with silence, resting in divine presence.

Couples who pray together build a love that cannot be broken one that is not just emotional, but spiritual, eternal.

5. Writing Your Own Love Language: Every couple has their unique way of speaking love. Create words, phrases, and affirmations that belong only to you.

A phrase only the two of you understand.

A whispered secret in the dark. A single word that, when spoken, brings you back to each other instantly.

These become anchors of love, small rituals of devotion that strengthen connection over time.

Final Thought:

Love is Spoken into Existence What you speak into your relationship, you create. What you affirm, you strengthen.

What you whisper, you ignite. What you pray over, you protect.

Love is not only felt. It must be declared, nurtured, and spoken into existence daily.

Speak your love, breathe it, and devote yourself to it. Let your words be the foundation of something eternal.

Love is not only felt; it must be declared, nurtured, and spoken into existence daily.

Speak your love, breathe it, and devote yourself to it. Let your words be the foundation of something eternal.

The Art of Speaking and Listening Building a Foundation Through Words

Words are not just expressions; they are the bricks that build the foundation of love. Every word spoken to your partner either strengthens the bond or weakens it. Love requires language, but even more than that, it requires deep listening.

Always create words that build a strong foundation. Words should be spoken with care, with the intention to uplift, to reassure, to nourish the soul. A relationship built on words of affirmation, truth, and love will stand strong, even in the face of challenges.

At the same time, practice listening, not just to respond, but to understand. What does your partner need to hear?

What are they truly saying, beyond their words?

Are they longing for reassurance, acknowledgment, or deeper connection?

True intimacy is found in knowing what to say and when to say nothing at all. Some words are meant to be spoken; others are meant to be felt.

Before speaking, ask yourself:

Is this word adding love to our foundation? Am I listening to what my partner truly needs?

Can I offer comfort in a way that nurtures their heart?

When couples master both speaking and listening, love deepens, intimacy flourishes, and the relationship becomes unshakable.

The Art of Deep Listening: A Ritual for Understanding Each Other's Needs Love is not just about what is said but also what is heard. True intimacy requires listening with the heart, not just the ears tuning into what your partner needs, even when they struggle to express it.

This ritual is designed to deepen connection through intentional listening, creating a space where both partners feel seen, heard, and fully understood.

The Sacred Listening Ritual

Step 1: Create a Listening Space

Choose a quiet, comfortable place where you can be fully present with each other. Remove distractions, no phones, no TV, no outside noise.

Sit close, holding hands or touching in some way to create energetic connection. Step 2: The Practice of Heartfelt Listening

1. One partner speaks first. Share whatever is on your heart, something you need, something weighing on you, or simply what you feel.

2. The other partner's role is to listen without interrupting, without thinking about how to respond only absorbing, feeling, and receiving.

3. Once the speaker is finished, the listener repeats back what they heard in their own words:

   "What I hear you saying is" … "I feel that you need" …

   "Sounds like this is important to you because" …

4. The speaker confirms if they feel truly understood. If not, they can clarify.

This step ensures that both partners feel completely heard, not just on the surface, but in the depth of their emotions.

Step 3: Offering Words That Nurture

Once understanding is reached, the listener responds not with solutions, not with fixing, but with love.

If your partner is seeking reassurance, offer words that affirm their worth and importance. If they are in pain, respond with comfort and presence.

If they are longing for connection, offer a touch, a word, or a simple moment of closeness.

Examples of nurturing responses:

I hear you, and I want you to know I am here for you.

You don't have to carry this alone. I am with you. I appreciate you sharing this with me; your feelings matter.

Sometimes, no words are needed at all. And just holding each other in silence can be more powerful than anything spoken.

Step 4: Sealing the Connection

Once both partners have spoken and been heard, seal the ritual with a physical gesture: A long embrace.

Forehead to forehead, breathing in sync.

Holding hands in stillness, letting the energy of love settle between you. Speak one final affirmation to reinforce the strength of your love:

We are here for each other, always.

Our love is a place of safety, where we are seen and understood. No matter what, we choose love again and again.

By ending in a peaceful connection, you strengthen the foundation of your relationship, ensuring that love is always heard, always felt, always nurtured.

Why This Ritual Matters

Many conflicts arise not because of disagreement, but because of feeling unheard. Deep listening strengthens trust, intimacy, and emotional security in a relationship.

When partners practice listening with love, they naturally begin to speak with love as well.

Love is not just in the words you say, but in the space, you create for each other to be fully heard.

Chapter 18
The Sacred Seasons of Love: Honoring the Cycles of Intimacy

Love, like nature, moves in seasons and cycles it is not meant to remain the same, but to flow, evolve, and shift over time. Just as there are times of intense passion, there are also times of quiet connection, deep emotional bonding, and necessary rest.

When couples understand the natural rhythms of love, they stop fearing change and instead learn to embrace each phase as sacred. Every season of love has its purpose, and when honored, it strengthens intimacy rather than weakens it.

This chapter explores how to:

Recognize and honor the different seasons of love.

Understand that love is not just about passion, but also about depth, trust, and renewal. Move through seasons without fear, allowing each phase to nurture your connection.

1. The Four Sacred Seasons of Love

1. Spring A the Season of Newness & Awakening

A time of new beginnings, discovery, and excitement.

Love feels alive, fresh, and full of possibility whether it's a new relationship or a renewal in an existing one.

Energy is high, intimacy is effortless, and emotions are overflowing.

This is the season of exploration, deep conversations, and spontaneous affection.

How to Honor Spring:

Try new experiences together. Express love openly, with excitement.

Set intentions for what you want to cultivate in your relationship.

2. Summer is The Season of Passion & Deep Connection
   The fire of love burns bright.

Physical, emotional, and spiritual intimacy are heightened. Love-making is deep, expressive, and overflowing with passion.

This is the season of strength, confidence, and fully embracing each other's essence.

How to Honor Summer:

Prioritize sensuality and passion, keep the fire alive with touch, words, and presence. Be adventurous in your intimacy.

Celebrate your love allow yourselves to fully indulge in one another.

3. Autumn is The Season of Change and & Reflection, A time of transition, slowing down, and deepening emotional intimacy.

The fiery passion of summer shifts into something softer, more mature, more reflective. Couples may face challenges, old wounds, or a need to realign their connection.

This is the season of communication, patience, and intentional love.

How to Honor Autumn: Have honest, vulnerable conversations. Reflect on the growth of your relationship.

Be gentle with each other, love through change, rather than resisting it.

4. Winter is The Season of Stillness & Deep Rest. A season of quiet intimacy, comfort, and trust. Love-making may slow down, but deep emotional and spiritual connection grow stronger.

A time to rest in love, rather than chase passion. This is the season of holding each other close, offering stability, and finding peace in simply being together.

How to Honor Winter:

Embrace slow intimacy, soft touches, quiet nights, whispered words. Find joy in stillness. Love does not always need to be loud to be real. Trust that even in rest, love is growing.

2. Moving Through the Seasons Without Fear

Many couples struggle when they feel their love shifting. They fear the loss of passion, the quiet moments, the changes that come with time.

But love is not meant to remain in one state forever. A fire that burns too hot without rest will burn out. A flower that never changes will not grow. Love, when allowed to move naturally, becomes deeper, richer, and more eternal.

Questions for Reflection:

What season do you feel your relationship is in right now?

Have you ever resisted a shift in seasons, fearing what it meant?

How can you embrace the phase you are in, rather than trying to force something different?

3. The Ritual of Seasonal Love Renewal

This ritual is designed to help couples recognize, honor, and move through their current season of love, allowing it to strengthen intimacy rather than create fear or distance.

How to Perform the Seasonal Love Ritual:

1. Sit together and reflect on what season you are currently in.

Is your love in a stage of fire and passion, or a stage of stillness and depth? Are you experiencing renewal, intensity, transition, or quiet devotion?

2. Express appreciation for the gifts of this season.

If in Spring: I love the new energy we are creating together. If in Summer: cherish the passion we are experiencing.

If in Autumn: I honor the depth and reflection we are moving through. If in Winter: I find peace in the stillness of our love.

3. Set an intention for the season ahead. What do you want to embrace more fully?

How can you love more deeply in this season?

4. Seal the ritual with a physical connection.

A deep embrace, a slow dance, a shared prayer, or an intimate moment of closeness.

By honoring where love is naturally flowing, couples create peace rather than resistance, trust rather than fear.

Final Thought:

Love is Eternal, But Its Expression Changes Love is not defined by a single moment it is a lifetime of seasons, each one necessary, each one beautiful.

Spring teaches us to be open to newness. Summer teaches us to embrace passion fully. Autumn teaches us to surrender to change.

Winter teaches us to rest in trust.

No matter what season you are in, know that love is always present, always growing, always deepening, always preparing you for the next phase.

Embrace it. Move with it. Love is sacred in every season.

The Reflection of Life's Sacred Love as Nature's Rhythm

Sacred love is like a reflection of life itself. It moves, shifts, and evolves, just as the world around us does.

Think of the ocean waves and the shoreline they are never truly separated. The waves may rise and fall, they may pull away only to return again, but their connection is eternal. The ocean never stops reaching for the shore, and the shore never stops welcoming the ocean home.

This is how love should be a continuous, flowing connection that is never truly broken, only moving in harmony with life's rhythm.

To deepen love, view it as a force of nature:

Love should be as vast and endless as the ocean, capable of carrying passion, depth, and renewal.

Love should be as steady as the mountains, offering unwavering trust and security.

Love should be as nourishing as the rain, bringing life to intimacy, to connection, to growth. Love should be as rooted as the earth, strong enough to weather any storm.

1. Feeling Love as a Living Energy

Love is not just an emotion, it is a force, a presence, a living energy that is constantly moving through you.

Close your eyes. Feel your love like an ocean wave. Does it crash with intensity, or does it flow gently toward the shore?

Imagine your love as the wind unseen, yet always felt. How does it move between you?

Let love be a fire, but also let it be water. Learn to embrace both passion and calm.

When you tune into love as a natural element, it becomes easier to trust its movements to know that even in quiet moments, even in shifts, love is always present.

2. The Ritual of Natural Love is Connecting Through Earths Elements

This practice helps couples align their love with the natural world, strengthening their connection by viewing their relationship as part of something eternal.

How to Perform the Nature Connection Ritual:

1. Choose a natural setting by the ocean, in the forest, near a river, or even in your own home where you can be grounded.

2. Stand or sit together, holding hands. Close your eyes and breathe in the energy of nature.

3. Reflect on how your love mirrors the world around you. Our love moves like the tides, always returning to each

other. Our connection is like the wind felt even when unseen.

Like fire, our passion burns, and like the earth, our love remains steady.

4. Speak your commitment to each other, inspired by natures strength:

I will love you as the ocean loves the shoreline forever reaching, forever returning. I will stand by you like the mountains unshaken, unwavering.

I will be the air that fills your breath, the warmth that surrounds you, the calm after the storm.

5. Seal the ritual with an embrace, a deep gaze, or a moment of stillness.

By aligning love with something greater than yourselves, it becomes unshakable, limitless, and deeply rooted in life itself.

3. Trusting Loves Cycles, Like the Moon, Like the Tide

Just as the moon guides the tides, love follows a natural cycle.

Some nights, the moon is full, illuminating everything. These are the moments when passion is high and when love feels effortless and abundant.

Other nights, the moon is hidden, but it is still there. Love does not disappear in quiet moments; it is simply resting, renewing, and preparing to rise again.

When you understand that love, like the ocean and the moon, follows its own rhythm, you stop resisting change. Instead, you surrender to the natural flow of intimacy, passion, and devotion.

Trust that even in stillness, love is alive. Even in distance, love is returning. Even in darkness, love is waiting to rise.

Final Thought:

Love is the Most Natural Thing in the World Just as the ocean never stops touching the shore, love never truly leaves.

Just as the earth holds steady beneath the weight of time, love remains when it is rooted in something deeper than the surface.

Just as nature moves in rhythms of passion and peace, intensity and stillness, love follows the same sacred flow.

Let your love be as strong as the tide, as constant as the moon, as natural as the wind, and as eternal as the earth itself.

Chapter 19
The Dances of Love: Moving in Divine Rhythm

Love, in its purest form, is a dance a silent conversation between two souls moving in harmony. Just as music carries rhythm and energy, so too does intimacy. The way two lovers move together, breathe together, and feel each other without words is a sacred art.

There are melodies, just instrumental, called "Divine Music", sounds that stimulate the senses, awaken the body, and create a shared frequency between lovers. This is not about technique or choreography; it is about feeling, flowing, and merging into one rhythm.

In this chapter, we will explore the sacred practice of dancing as a form of love-making, energy alignment, and deep sensual connection.

1. The Sacred Dance of Frequency, Moving Without Touch

One of the most profound ways to connect with your partner is to move in sync without touch to let the energy between you create the bond, rather than physical contact.

How to Perform the Divine Music Dance

1. Choose a piece of instrumental music, something rhythmic, something sensual, something that stimulates the senses.

2. Stand a few inches apart, facing each other.

3. Close your eyes for a moment and breathe. Feel your energy begin to merge.

4. Open your eyes and hold steady eye contact.

5. Let the music move through you, not thinking, not forcing, just feeling.

6. Begin to sway, step, and flow together, without speaking, without touching, just existing in the same rhythm.

7. Notice how, without effort, your movements begin to align. You are not just dancing. You are becoming the same frequency.

This can be a deeply sensual experience not because of proximity but because of the intensity of the connection. When two people synchronize their movements without needing to hold each other, they create an unspoken language, a shared vibration, a union beyond the physical.

2. The Fire and Water of Dance: Two Forms of Intimacy

Dancing is not just about passion; it is about balance. Some dances are wild, fiery, full of intensity; others are soft, slow, deeply intimate.

The Fire Dance is fast, primal, and uninhibited. A celebration of energy, of attraction, of raw emotion.

The Water Dance is slow, fluid, and intentional. A movement of deep trust, surrender, and presence.

A sacred relationship holds both. Love-making mirrors this balance sometimes it is fire, sometimes it is water, but it is always a dance.

Practice: The Shift Between Fire and Water

1. Begin the dance with fire, quick steps, bold movements, intense eye contact.

2. Slowly transition into water, slowing down, softening, melting into the rhythm.

3. Notice how the energy shifts, how passion and peace are not separate, but part of the same movement.

4. End in stillness, breathing, looking, and existing in the energy you have created together.

This practice teaches lovers to read each other's energy, to sense the natural flow between passion and stillness, between movement and surrender.

3. Dancing as Foreplay: Awakening the Body Before Touch

Touch is powerful, but there is something equally intoxicating about feeling desire built before it is satisfied. Dancing allows energy to rise, to tease, to pull, to awaken the senses in a way that deepens intimacy beyond just the physical.

The Sensual Dance Ritual

1. Set the atmosphere low lights, candles, deep earthy scents (like sandalwood or jasmine).

2. Choose a song that calls to the body something rich in rhythm, something slow but hypnotic.

3. Begin apart, allowing distance to create anticipation.

4. Move with intention, not rushing to touch, but letting the space between you be the most charged place in the room.

5. When the moment feels right, close the space slowly, deliberately, allowing touch to become an extension of the music.

By the time you touch, your bodies are already attuned to one another, vibrating at the same frequency, fully immersed in connection.

4. Dance as Worship: Sacred Movement Beyond Passion

There is a reason dance has been a spiritual practice in cultures for centuries, it is one of the purest ways to express love, devotion, and surrender.

A slow dance with your lover is not just romantic; it is a form of worship, a way to honor the body, the connection, and the divine presence within your love.

The Dance of Devotion

1. Begin by holding each other, foreheads touching, in stillness.

2. Breathe together, aligning your energy.

3. Let movement come naturally, whether slow, swaying, or stepping in rhythm.

4. As you move, whisper words of love, gratitude, and devotion into each other's ears.

5. Let the dance be a meditation, a prayer, a physical expression of the depth of your union.

This is the kind of movement that goes beyond passion, it seals the bond between souls, making love a living, breathing force.

5. The Rhythm of Love: Staying in Sync Beyond the Dance

The way couples dance together is often a reflection of how they move together in life. If you learn to trust the rhythm, to feel each other's energy, to move without force but with flow, love becomes effortless.

Even outside the dance, the principles remain:

Feel your partners energy before reacting.

Move with, not against, the natural rhythm of love.

Let passion and stillness be equal parts of the experience.

Trust that love, like music, is not meant to be controlled only felt, surrendered to, and embraced.

Final Thought:

Love is a Dance That Never Ends Every touch, every breath, every moment spent moving together is a dance. Some dances are filled with fire, some are filled with peace, but all are sacred when done in love.

Dance together often. Dance in joy. Dance in passion. Dance in stillness.

But most importantly, we should never stop moving to the rhythm of each other's love.

Chapter 20
Intentional Eating: Nourishing Love Through Sacred Consumption

The way we eat is just as important as what we eat. Food is not just fuel, it is energy, vibration, a form of connection to both the body and the soul. When approached with intention, eating can become a sacred practice, deepening intimacy between partners and aligning love with nourishment.

Eating with love, presence, and awareness transforms meals from routine consumption to an act of devotion, a way to honor the body, nurture the relationship, and align with divine energy.

This chapter explores how intentional eating can deepen love, how food and sensuality are intertwined, and how the act of eating can be a practice in presence, gratitude, and sacred connection.

1. The Sacred Relationship Between Food and Love

Food has always been a symbol of love, unity, and sensuality. Sharing a meal is an act of offering, of communion.

The act of feeding your partner is an intimate gesture of care.

Certain foods awaken the senses, increase desire, and deepen physical connection.

When approached with intention, eating becomes an extension of love-making, of presence, of honoring each other's well-being.

Ask yourself:

Do we eat with presence, or are we distracted?

Are we nourishing our bodies in a way that supports our love?

Do we approach food with gratitude or simply as something to consume?

When couples begin to see food as sacred, it naturally deepens their intimacy, health, and emotional connection.

2. The Practice of Intentional Eating, Bringing Awareness to Meals

Most people eat without thought, without presence, without connection to their food or their partner. Intentional eating is about slowing down, tuning in, and transforming meals into a shared, sensual experience.

The Ritual of Intentional Eating

1. Prepare the meal together: Cooking can be an act of love, a moment of connection before the meal itself.

2. Create a sacred space, Dim the lights, light candles, play soft music. Make the environment one of peace and presence.

3. Before eating, take a moment of gratitude, hold hands, close your eyes, and express thanks for the food, the nourishment, and the love you share.

4. Eat slowly, without distractions. Savor every bite. Notice the textures, flavors, and sensations.

5. Feed each other occasionally, not for necessity, but as a gentle reminder that food is an offering of love.

6. End with appreciation: A simple Thank you for sharing this meal with me strengthens connection.

Eating in this way heightens awareness, deepens gratitude, and brings couples into full presence with one another.

3. Food and Sensuality: Awakening the Senses Through Nourishment

Certain foods are known to heighten sensuality, increase pleasure, and enhance intimacy. When eaten intentionally, they can activate desire, stimulate the senses, and prepare the body for deeper connection.

Foods That Awaken Love & Sensuality:

Dark Chocolate: Releases endorphins, creating pleasure and relaxation.

Figs & Strawberries Naturally sensual, enhancing desire through taste and texture. Avocado & Nuts Nourish the body with healthy fats that enhance skin sensitivity. Honey & Cinnamon: Increase warmth, circulation, and natural attraction.

145

Wine or Herbal Teas: Slows down the moment, allowing relaxation and presence.

Sensual Eating Practice

1. Choose a food to share: a piece of fruit, chocolate, or something rich in texture.

2. Take turns feeding each other slowly and intentionally.

3. Stay in eye contact, tuning into how each bite feels and how the body reacts.

4. Let the act of eating become foreplay, building intimacy through shared pleasure.

By merging food and sensuality, eating becomes a bridge between nourishment and love- making, deepening the physical and emotional bond between lovers.

4. Aligning Food with Energy & Love's Rhythm

Food is not just physical. It carries energy, frequency, and intention. Eating foods that align with your relationship's rhythm can strengthen love and well-being.

Grounding Foods (Root Vegetables, Nuts, Whole Grains) Strengthen emotional stability and trust.

High-Energy Foods (Fresh Fruits, Raw Honey, Herbs) Enhance passion and vitality.

Cleansing Foods (Leafy Greens, Herbal Teas, Citrus) Clear negative energy and refresh intimacy.

Comforting Foods (Warm Soups, Stews, Baked Goods) Bring a sense of peace, nurturing, and deep connection.

By choosing foods with intention and awareness, couples can align their love with the energy of what they consume, creating balance in both body and spirit.

5. Fasting & Feasting: The Balance of Restraint & Indulgence in Love

Just as in intimacy, balance is needed between holding back and indulging fully.

Fasting together (whether from food or external distractions) creates a deeper appreciation for nourishment, making meals even more sacred.

Feasting with intention, not overeating, but fully enjoying, savoring, and celebrating love through food.

Learning to listen to the body knowing when it needs cleansing, when it needs pleasure, and when it needs rest.

A couple that practices balance in nourishment also learns balance in love knowing when to hold back, when to indulge, and when to simply be present in the moment.

The Final Thought:

Eating as an Act of Love Eating is not just about survival. It is a sacred exchange of energy, a way to honor the body, and a way to nourish love.

The more presence and awareness brought into meals, the deeper intimacy and connection grow.

When approached with intention, food becomes more than nourishment; it becomes an offering, a ritual, a way to love.

Eat with love, feed each other with devotion, and let nourishment be a sacred part of intimacy.

Would you like to add a personal experience or specific foods that hold deep meaning in love and intimacy for you?

The Symbolism & Energy of Eggs in Love & Intimacy

Across many cultures, eggs have been seen as symbols of life, fertility, creation, and renewal. In the context of intentional eating and sacred love, eggs hold deep meaning both spiritually and physically.

Creation & Fertility Eggs represent new beginnings, the potential for life, and the energy of creation. In a relationship, they symbolize the continuous renewal of love, the deepening of intimacy, and the cycle of growth within a sacred union.

Balance of Yin & Yang The egg's composition reflects divine balance:

The yolk (rich, golden, full of life) represents passion, warmth, desire, and the essence of love itself.

The white (pure, protective, structured) symbolizes nurturing energy, emotional depth, and stability.

Together, they represent the perfect merging of fire and stillness, passion and peace, the essence of sacred union.

Nourishment for Love & Sensuality: Eggs are known for their rich nutritional benefits that support intimacy:

High in protein, it Provides sustained energy, essential for physical endurance.

Rich in healthy fats and vitamins, it nourishes the skin, enhances the natural glow, and supports hormonal balance.

Boosts brain function & mood: Helps in reducing stress and increasing emotional well- being, leading to a deeper connection between partners.

Using Eggs in Intentional Eating for Love

Because of their deep symbolic and energetic significance, eggs can be meaningfully incorporated into sacred eating rituals.

1. The Egg as a Morning Ritual for Love

Sharing eggs at breakfast together can be a practice of starting the day in harmony. Before eating, pause to acknowledge the egg's energy of renewal and nourishment. Whisper a simple affirmation:

As we eat, we nourish our love, our bodies, and our connection.

Cook them with intention, whether soft and delicate or rich and indulgent, allowing the texture to match your energy.

2. Eggs & Sensuality: A Food of Texture & Pleasure

The experience of eating eggs can be deeply sensual if approached with presence:

A soft-boiled egg has a luxurious, slow-moving texture, teaching patience and appreciation.

A poached egg drapes over food, mimicking the fluidity of love, the way passion melts into surrender.

A fried egg with a runny yolk represents richness, indulgence, and the desire to be fully immersed in pleasure.

By sharing eggs with your partner in a moment of stillness, you allow food to become a sensory experience, deepening both your appreciation for each other and the act of nourishment.

3. Eggs & Fertility: A Symbolic Ritual for Couples Wanting to Create Together

For couples on a journey of deepening their union, conceiving life, or creating something meaningful together, eggs can serve as a symbol of shared intention.

Prepare eggs together, being mindful of the energy you are infusing into them.

Speak or write down an intention, not just for physical fertility, but for the birth of new love, new experiences, and new beginnings.

Eat in silence, allowing the energy of creation to be felt between you.

Even beyond physical fertility, this practice symbolizes the birth of new cycles, growth, and transformation within love itself.

Final Thought:

Eggs as a Reflection of Sacred Love Eggs, in their simplicity, carry the essence of life, nourishment, and balance. Whether shared over a slow breakfast, eaten as a sensual experience, or honored for their symbolism of renewal, they remind us that:

Love is like an egg: strong and delicate, requiring care and intention.

Nourishment is not just about feeding the body. It is about feeding love, energy, and connection.

When approached with presence, every meal can become an act of devotion, a ritual of intimacy, and a moment of sacred exchange.

The Sacred Power of Honey: Nourishing Love & Spirit

Honey is more than just a sweetener, it is a divine elixir, a symbol of wisdom, abundance, healing, and sacred love. In many spiritual traditions, honey represents the richness of divine blessings, the sweetness of life, and the depth of intimacy when shared with intention.

In the context of sacred union, honey is a gift of nature that can enhance love, connection, and nourishment, both physically and spiritually. It holds healing properties, carries the essence of the flowers it comes from, and has been used in rituals, offerings, and love- making throughout history.

Ways to Use Honey with Intention

1. As a Blessing for Love & Marriage

In biblical and ancient traditions, honey symbolized divine favor and abundance. It was often given as a wedding gift or consumed as a symbol of a blessed union.

To bless your relationship, you can:

Stir a little honey into tea and pray over it, setting an intention for sweetness, unity, and divine love in your relationship.

Write a prayer or affirmation for your union, dip it in honey, and bury it in the earth as a symbol of planting love that grows.

2. As a Sacred Food for Nourishing Love & Intimacy

Honey is a natural aphrodisiac, known to enhance vitality, passion, and sensual connection. You can incorporate honey into meals shared with your beloved:

Drizzle honey over fruits like figs, dates, or pomegranate, foods of passion and fertility.

Add honey to herbal teas that promote relaxation, heart-opening, and connection (such as rose, cinnamon, or chamomile).

Prepare a honey-based dessert together as an act of shared creation and intimacy.

3. In Love-Making & Sensory Awakening

Honey has been used in love rituals to heighten the senses and create a deeper connection. Some ways to use honey in sacred intimacy:

Taste & Touch: Feeding each other honey can be an intimate and playful act of nourishing one another in love.

Massage & Anointing: Mixing honey with warm oil (such as olive or coconut) and massaging your beloved can be a form of healing touch and devotion.

Symbolic Offering: Placing a small amount of honey on the lips as a sign of speaking love, sweetness, and truth into your union.

4. As a Spiritual Cleanser & Healing Elixir

Honey is naturally purifying and has been used for centuries in cleansing and healing rituals.

Ways to use honey for purification:

Mix honey with warm water and drink it in the morning as a cleansing ritual to invite divine wisdom and clarity.

Use honey in skin care, apply a thin layer to your face or body and wash with warm water, imagining any negative energy being released.

Anoint your heart or forehead with honey during prayer or meditation as a symbol of receiving divine wisdom and love.

5. In Fasting, Feasting, & Rhythms of Nourishment

Honey can be part of both fasting and feasting, aligning with the natural cycles of nourishment.

During fasting, a small amount of honey in water can sustain energy while keeping the mind clear and spiritually attuned.

During feasting, honey represents abundance, used in special meals, desserts, or sacred offerings.

Bringing Honey into Your Life with Purpose: To use honey as a sacred element in your relationship and personal nourishment:

Always choose pure, raw honey, the closer to nature, the higher its spiritual and healing properties.

Eat honey with intention, not just as food, but as an act of receiving divine sweetness in your life.

Use honey to bless your relationship, whether in shared meals, intimate moments, or love rituals.

Speak love over honey before consuming it, asking for its energy to bring sweetness and wisdom to your journey.

Honey is more than just a substance; it is a symbol of God's overflowing love and the sacred joy of intimacy.

When used with awareness, it becomes a tool for nourishment, healing, and deepening love.

The Sacred Symbolism of Apples: Nourishment, Wisdom & Love Apples are one of the most deeply symbolic fruits in spiritual and romantic traditions. They represent wisdom, divine knowledge, love, fertility, passion, and sacred union. Throughout history, apples have been seen as a bridge between earthly pleasure and spiritual enlightenment.

In the context of sacred intimacy and nourishment, apples hold profound meaning. They are a fruit of temptation, transformation, and divine sweetness, offering both the knowledge of self and the ability to deepen love through intention.

The Spiritual Meaning of Apples

1. A Fruit of Wisdom & Knowledge

In biblical and mythological traditions, apples symbolize the pursuit of wisdom and divine truth.

The story of Adam and Eve often associates the apple with the knowledge of good and evil, representing the awakening of awareness.

Eating an apple with intention can be a ritual of seeking wisdom, an act of opening oneself to divine truth and understanding in love.

2. A Symbol of Love & Sacred Union

Apples have long been associated with romantic love, passion, and eternal devotion.

In ancient Greece, an apple was offered as a declaration of love, if accepted, it symbolized a bond of commitment and unity.

Sharing an apple with a beloved can represent choosing one another in love, growth, and spiritual connection.

3. Fertility, Creation & the Womb

The apple's round shape and seeds within make it a symbol of fertility, abundance, and the womb of creation.

In sacred intimacy, apples represent the birthing of new energy, new life, and the cyclical nature of love.

Eating apples with awareness can be a way to honor the fruitfulness of love, both in the physical and spiritual realms.

4. Balance Between Pleasure & Discipline

Apples are both sweet and crisp, offering a balance between delight and structure, indulgence and wisdom.

Just as love requires both passion and commitment, the apple reminds us that true nourishment comes from embracing both pleasure and sacred responsibility.

Eating an apple slowly, savoring each bite, can be a meditation on the balance of passion and patience in love.

Ways to Use Apples with Intention

1. As a Love Ritual

Share an apple with your beloved, taking turns biting into it is a symbolic act of unity, commitment, and shared destiny.

Bake apples into a dessert together, a sensual way to co-create nourishment in love.

Offer an apple as a gift of devotion, just as ancient lovers did to express love and commitment.

2. As a Symbol of Wisdom & Reflection

Before eating an apple, ask for wisdom, whether in love, relationships, or personal growth.

Write a question on a piece of paper and place it beneath an apple overnight. In the morning, eat the apple while reflecting on the answer that may come to you.

If seeking guidance in love, hold an apple in your hands, close your eyes, and set an intention before taking the first bite.

3. As a Food for Sacred Intimacy

Apples are filled with life-giving nutrients that nourish the body, awaken energy, and enhance vitality.

Pair apples with honey or cinnamon, both known for their aphrodisiac and heart-opening properties.

Use apples as part of a romantic meal or a sacred union ceremony, symbolizing the sweetness and depth of your connection.

4. As a Tool for Letting Go & Renewal

Just as apples fall from trees in autumn, they remind us of the beauty of release, surrender, and renewal.

If holding onto past wounds, write them on a piece of paper, place it near an apple, and as you eat the apple, visualize yourself letting go and making space for new love and wisdom.

In moments of transition, eat an apple mindfully as a ritual of new beginnings, transformation, and divine nourishment.

Bringing Apples into Your Life with Purpose

Eat apples with presence, savoring their sweetness as a reminder of life's blessings.

Use apples as a ritual of love, unity, and commitment in relationships.

See apples as a symbol of balance between pleasure and wisdom, passion and patience. Honor apples as a sacred fruit of creation, nourishment, and transformation.

Apples are more than food, they are a reflection of life's mysteries, the beauty of love, and the wisdom of divine nourishment. When eaten with intention, they become a sacred offering, a way to nourish not just the body but also the heart, the soul, and the love we share.

The Sacred Nourishment of Cucumber, Radish, and Spinach

Each food carries its own spiritual frequency, energy, and symbolism. In the context of sacred nourishment, love, and vitality, these three foods, cucumber, radish, and spinach, represent hydration, cleansing, passion, renewal, and strength. When eaten with intention, they become more than just physical nourishment; they align the body and soul with divine energy, preparing one for deeper intimacy, love, and connection.

Cucumber: Hydration, Purity & Cooling Energy Symbolism & Spiritual Significance Hydration & Renewal: Cucumbers are water-rich, representing emotional balance, purification, and clarity. Just as water cleanses and refreshes, cucumber brings cooling energy, restoring the body's flow.

Calm & Soothing Presence: In relationships, cucumber represents a soft, calming love, one that nurtures rather than overwhelms.

Fertility & Growth: The shape of cucumbers has often been linked to fertility, abundance, and masculine energy in sacred traditions.

How to Use Cucumber with Intention

Eat cucumber when you need emotional cleansing and renewal.

Make a refreshing cucumber-infused water, speaking love and purity into it before drinking.

Share a cooling cucumber-based dish with your partner to symbolize balance, peace, and renewal in love.

Use cucumber slices in skincare as a ritual of self-love, releasing tension and refreshing your energy.

Radish: Passion, Vitality & Awakening

Symbolism & Spiritual Significance

Fire & Passion: Radishes have a naturally spicy, invigorating taste, representing heat, passion, and awakening energy. They symbolize the spark of desire, courage, and boldness in love.

Detoxification & Purification: Radishes cleanse the blood and body, aligning with the energy of shedding what no longer serves, releasing old wounds, and stepping into renewed love.

Transformation & Hidden Strength: Radishes grow underground, reminding us that real change happens within before it emerges outwardly. In relationships, this symbolizes depth, unseen passion, and transformation beneath the surface.

How to Use Radish with Intention Eat radish when you want to ignite passion, excitement, and vitality in your relationship.

Use radishes in a shared meal to symbolize uncovering deep emotions and embracing hidden desires.

Meditate before eating radish, setting an intention to release emotional toxins and step into new energy.

Pair radish with honey or cucumber to balance passion with gentleness fire with coolness. Spinach: Strength, Nourishment & Heart-Opening Energy

Symbolism & Spiritual Significance

Strength & Endurance: Spinach is a powerful, nutrient-dense food representing inner strength, resilience, and fortification. It reminds us that true love and intimacy require nourishment and care.

Heart-Opening & Emotional Healing: The rich green color of spinach aligns with the heart chakra, supporting emotional balance, love, and the ability to give and receive affection freely.

Grounded Energy & Vitality Spinach grows close to the earth, carrying the energy of stability, renewal, and deep-rooted nourishment.

How to Use Spinach with Intention Eat spinach when you need emotional or physical strength in your relationship.

Make a spinach-based meal with your partner as a way to nurture each other's hearts and souls.

Drink a green smoothie with spinach, setting an intention to fortify your love and deepen your connection.

Use spinach as a symbol of renewal, grounding, and embracing nourishment in all forms. Bringing These Foods into Your Life with Purpose

Cucumber cools and purifies; it helps maintain balance, ease tension, and cleanse emotions. Radish ignites and awakens; it brings passion, clarity, and energy to love and life.

Spinach strengthens and nourishes; it fortifies the heart, body, and soul for lasting love.

Prunes: The Sacred Fruit of Purification, Longevity & Deep Nourishment

Prunes dried plums are often overlooked, yet they carry profound spiritual, emotional, and physical significance. They symbolize purification, longevity, deep nourishment, and the release of what no longer serves us. Their rich, dark color and deeply concentrated sweetness remind us that true nourishment often comes from what has been refined, aged, and made stronger through time.

The Spiritual Meaning of Prunes

1. Purification & Release

Prunes are known for their natural cleansing properties, symbolizing the release of emotional, physical, and energetic burdens.

Just as they help the body eliminate toxins, they also serve as a reminder that we must let go of what weighs us down in love and life to make space for renewal.

Eating prunes with intention can be a ritual for emotional detoxification, letting go of past wounds, resentment, or anything that blocks intimacy and love.

2. Longevity & Wisdom

In many cultures, dried fruits represent preservation and wisdom gained over time.

Prunes symbolize the beauty of lasting love, endurance, and the richness that comes from deep spiritual connection.

Just as prunes become sweeter and richer with time, so does a relationship that is nurtured with patience, care, and devotion.

3. Deep Nourishment & Grounding Energy

Prunes are packed with iron, fiber, and minerals, providing deep physical and energetic nourishment.

They are grounding, stabilizing, and replenishing, making them a powerful food for reconnecting with the body, balancing emotions, and finding inner peace.

Their richness reminds us that true nourishment is not always fast or superficial, it requires depth, patience, and care.

4. Fertility & Sexual Vitality

In some traditions, prunes are associated with fertility, vitality, and reproductive health.

Their deep color and dense nutrients support life-force energy, making them an excellent food for those seeking to enhance physical stamina, passion, and connection in sacred union.

In love-making, prunes symbolize the ability to sustain energy, deepen intimacy, and nourish the body for lasting pleasure.

Ways to Use Prunes with Intention

1. As a Ritual for Letting Go & Emotional Cleansing

Eat a prune mindfully, setting the intention to release anything heavy in your heart.

Pair prunes with warm herbal tea, allowing yourself to reflect on what needs to be released in love or life.

Write down an emotion or burden on paper, eat a prune as a symbol of cleansing, and burn or bury the paper as a letting-go ritual.

2. As a Food for Longevity & Lasting Love

Share prunes with your partner as a symbol of commitment, endurance, and deep connection that grows richer over time.

Use prunes in a dish that represents longevity, patience, and the beauty of love that ages gracefully.

Drink prune juice as a sacred elixir of endurance and wisdom, honoring the process of slow, meaningful growth.

3. As Nourishment for Sacred Intimacy & Energy

Eat prunes as part of a diet that supports stamina, passion, and overall vitality in love- making.

Combine prunes with nuts, honey, and cinnamon to create an energy-enhancing snack that fuels both body and soul.

Use prunes in a meal before sacred intimacy as a reminder that love is about deep nourishment, not just surface pleasure.

Bringing Prunes into Your Life with Purpose

Eat prunes with awareness, using them as a tool for release, nourishment, and longevity.

Use prunes in meals as a reminder that patience, aging, and depth bring the greatest sweetness in love.

See prunes as a symbol of lasting energy, whether in relationships, spiritual growth, or personal vitality.

Let prunes be a sacred food of purification, wisdom, and renewal in both body and spirit.

Prunes teach us that true sweetness comes with time, that releasing what no longer serves us leads to renewal, and that deep nourishment is essential for lasting love.

Chapter 21
Growing Maintaining the Sacred Bond Through Transformation

Love is not meant to remain stagnant; it is meant to grow, evolve, and deepen. Just as nature changes with the seasons, so too do individuals and relationships. Growth is necessary, but if not handled with intention, it can create distance rather than deepen a connection.

The key to sustaining a sacred bond through growth is not resisting change but learning how to evolve together while holding onto the essence of your love. This chapter explores how to honor personal and relational growth without losing intimacy, connection, or devotion.

1. The Reality of Growth in Love

Every relationship will experience shifts, transitions, and periods of transformation. Growth can come in many forms: Spiritual Awakening: One partner may be evolving spiritually at a different pace.

Life Transitions Career shifts, parenthood, personal ambitions, or health changes. Emotional Deepening: Learning new truths about yourself or healing past wounds. Desires & Needs Shifting: What, once worked, may no longer feel fulfilling.

The most sacred relationships do not fear growth. They embrace it. They recognize that true love is not about staying the same but about continuously choosing each other in every new version of yourself.

2. Holding the Bond While Expanding Individually

One of the greatest challenges in love is learning how to grow without growing apart.

Sacred Practices to Stay Connected During Growth:

1. Daily Check-Ins. Even in times of change, keep communication open. Ask: What has been on your mind lately?

How do you feel about where we are right now? How can I support you in this season of growth?

Celebrate Each Other's Evolution Instead of fearing change, honor the new versions of each other.

2. Maintain Rituals of Connection: Even if personal growth is pulling you in different directions, keep sacred rituals intact (nightly touch, shared meals, quiet moments of presence).

3. Let Go of the Past Versions of Each Other. Honor who you were, but allow space for who you are becoming.

Love is not about holding onto a past version of your partner. It is about loving them in their becoming.

3. When One Person Grows Faster Than the Other

Not all growth happens at the same pace. Sometimes, one partner may be in a season of deep transformation while the other feels steady or unchanged.

If you are the one evolving: Be patient. Growth does not mean your partner is stagnant. It simply means they are moving at their own pace.

Share your journey without forcing them to follow the same path. Reassure them that your love is still strong, even as you change. If your partner is growing and you feel left behind:

Stay open and curious. Ask them about their journey, even if you don't fully understand it.

Release fear. Growth does not mean loss; it can mean deeper love if approached with trust.

Find ways to evolve together. Even if your paths look different, ask: How can we keep our bond strong in this process?

Growth is not a threat to love. It is an invitation to deepen love in new ways.

4. The Ritual of Renewal: Realigning Your Love Through Growth

This ritual is designed to help couples pause, reflect, and consciously realign their love as they grow individually.

How to Perform the Ritual of Renewal:

1. Sit facing each other in silence, holding hands.

2. Close your eyes and take a deep breath, feeling each other's presence.

3. One partner speaks first, expressing where they feel they are growing:

I feel myself changing in this way, learning this about myself

4. The other partner listens, then responds with support, I see you.

I honor your growth. I am here.

5. Switch roles, allowing both to express their transformations.

6. End by reaffirming your love in this season:

No matter how we grow, I choose you. Our love expands as we expand.

We are evolving, but we are still one.

By making growth a shared experience, couples move forward together rather than drifting apart.

The Final Thought:

Love That Expands is Love That Endures. Growth is not the end of love. It is the deepening of love.

True intimacy is not about staying the same but about continuously choosing each other in every stage of transformation.

When love is nurtured through growth, it becomes limitless, evolving into something even greater than before.

Let your love be as expansive as the universe, as adaptable as the ocean, and as eternal as the soul.

The Benefits of Growing Spiritually Together as a Couple When two people grow spiritually at the same time, their connection deepens on every level emotionally, mentally, physically, and energetically. A relationship rooted in shared spiritual evolution is one that is not just based on love but on a higher calling, a divine alignment, and an unshakable foundation.

Here are the key benefits of spiritual growth in unison:

1. A Deeper & Unbreakable Bond

When both partners evolve spiritually together, their energies become more aligned. They begin to see and understand each other beyond the physical realm. Their love transcends surface-level connection and becomes something divine.

They recognize each other's soul journey and offer unconditional support.

They share revelations, insights, and spiritual awakenings, bringing them closer. They become mirrors of growth, reflecting back wisdom and light to one another.

A couple that grows together spiritually is nearly unbreakable because their love is built on truth, purpose, and divine connection.

2. Communication Becomes Intuitive & Effortless

Spiritual alignment strengthens communication because it removes ego, fear, and misinterpretation from interactions.

Conversations shift from reactive to understanding and patient. They learn to listen with their hearts, not just their minds.

They speak with intention, using words that heal, uplift, and nurture.

Many times, they do not even need words. Their energies communicate naturally.

When couples grow spiritually together, they develop a telepathic-like connection, where they just know what the other feels, thinks, or needs without having to explain.

3. Love-Making Becomes a Sacred, Spiritual Experience

A couple that is spiritually aligned experiences a higher level of intimacy, where love- making becomes more than physical. It becomes an act of worship, a divine merging of souls.

Energy flows freely between them, making intimacy feel transcendent. They are fully present with each other, with no distractions or blockages.

Their love-making takes on a deeper meaning as it becomes a reflection of the divine.

When two people vibrate at the same spiritual frequency, their connection during intimacy is unmatched, often leading to heightened sensations, prolonged connection, and spiritual awakenings through love-making.

4. They Manifest Together: Powerful Co-Creation

A spiritually aligned couple shares the same vision for life, love, and purpose. Because of this, they become powerful manifestos together, able to attract and create anything they desire.

Their energy amplifies, making manifestations stronger.

They pray and set intentions together, aligning their desires with divine timing. Their connection to abundance, purpose, and fulfillment grows effortlessly.

A couple that prays, visualizes, and sets spiritual goals together will find that everything begins falling into place with ease. They become unstoppable.

5. Conflict Becomes a Tool for Growth, Not Destruction

When both partners are spiritually aligned, they see challenges not as threats but as opportunities for deepening their love.

Ego is removed from conflict. Instead of fighting, they seek to understand and heal.

They practice patience, forgiveness, and self-awareness, preventing unnecessary emotional wounds.

They focus on solutions, not problems, ensuring that every challenge strengthens rather than weakens their bond.

A spiritually awakened couple understands that love is bigger than any temporary argument. They resolve conflicts with wisdom, intention, and divine guidance.

6. They Hold Each Other Accountable for Growth & Higher Purpose

One of the most powerful benefits of spiritual alignment in a relationship is that each partner becomes a reflection of the other's highest self.

They call each other to greater levels of wisdom, love, and integrity.

They push each other beyond comfort zones, ensuring that neither settles for mediocrity.

They remind each other of their divine purpose, keeping them aligned with their soul's mission.

Instead of enabling bad habits or unhealthy cycles, they inspire each other to keep evolving, growing, and ascending.

7. The Relationship Feels Protected & Divinely Guided

When a couple grows spiritually together, their love is not just their own. It is divinely protected.

They feel guided by a higher power, sensing that their love is part of something greater.

They experience deep peace and security, knowing that their relationship is built on something unshakable.

They pray, meditate, and seek wisdom together, ensuring that they are always in alignment with divine will.

Because their love is rooted in spirit, it cannot be easily broken by external forces. They trust not just in each other but in the divine energy that holds them together.

Final Thought:

Love That Grows in Spirit is Love that lasts a couple that grows together spiritually does not fear change. They welcome it because they know that every step of growth is leading them to something greater.

Their love is not based on external things but on deep, inner alignment.

They see and love each other's souls beyond just the physical.

They move through life with a shared purpose, a shared vision, and a shared devotion.

This is the kind of love that transcends time, that becomes legendary, that serves as an example of what is truly possible when two souls evolve as one.

Practices for Spiritual Alignment as a Couple

How to Grow Spiritually Together and Strengthen Your Sacred Bond When two souls commit to growing spiritually together, their connection becomes stronger, deeper, and more aligned with divine energy. It is not enough to love one another. You must also build spiritual practices that keep you in harmony, elevate your consciousness, and align you with a shared purpose.

Here are powerful spiritual practices to help couples grow together while maintaining deep intimacy and connection.

1. Shared Meditation Synchronizing Your Energy

Meditation is one of the most powerful ways to align your energies, clear distractions, and merge into a single frequency.

How to Meditate Together:

1. Sit facing each other with your knees or hands touching.

2. Close your eyes and focus on your breath, letting your bodies relax.

3. Sync your breathing, inhale together, exhale together, until your rhythms align.

4. Visualize your energies merging as if a golden light is flowing between you.

5. Stay in this space of silence and connection, allowing your hearts and souls to communicate beyond words.

6. When finished, slowly open your eyes and hold each other's gaze, feeling the deep bond, you've created.

Why it works:

Enhances emotional and energetic connection.

Strengthens intuitive communication, allowing you to sense each other's feelings.

Clears negative energy and distractions, keeping the relationship centered.

2. Morning & Nightly Prayers: Anchoring Love in the Divine

A couple that prays together stays deeply connected because they invite divine energy into their relationship.

Morning Prayer: (Start the day with intention and unity.) Hold hands and say:

May this day bring us closer together in love, understanding, and divine purpose. Let us see each other with fresh eyes and hearts open to love.

Nightly Prayer: (Release stress and surrender to divine guidance.) Speak words of gratitude:

Thank you for another day of love and growth.

I bless you with peace, rest, and a heart full of love.

End with a moment of stillness, simply feeling each other's presence.

Why it works:

Deepens spiritual intimacy and strengthens trust. Brings peace and alignment before sleep.

Invites divine protection over your relationship.

3. Energy Healing & Touch Rituals

Physical touch is a powerful transmitter of energy. When used intentionally, it can heal, awaken, and align your partner's spirit.

How to Perform an Energy Healing Touch Ritual:

1. Sit in front of each other. One person places their hands over the other's heart.

2. Close your eyes and send loving energy. Visualize golden light flowing from your hands into their heart.

3. Speak healing affirmations:

I bless you with peace.

May your soul feel held and safe.

4. Switch roles and repeat.

5. End with a long, intentional embrace, allowing your energies to fully merge.

Why it works

Strengthens trust and emotional safety. Removes stress and emotional blocks.

Creates an unspoken bond of healing and support.

4. The Shared Manifestation Practice: Co-Creating Your Future

When couples align their vision for the future, they become powerful co-creators.

How to Manifest Together:

1. Sit together in a sacred space.

2. Write down your shared intentions (for your love, home, family, or spiritual growth).

3. Speak them aloud in unity, such as:

We attract a life of peace, love, and abundance.

We build a home filled with harmony and divine presence.

4. Visualize these desires as already real.

5. Seal the practice with gratitude, thanking the universe, God, or your higher selves for guiding you.

Why it works:

Align your visions, dreams, and goals as a couple.

Strengthens faith in each other's path and purpose.

Creates a shared energetic field of abundance and possibility.

5. Sacred Love-Making Merging Spirit, Mind & Body

Intimacy is not just physical. It is a spiritual exchange of energy, devotion, and oneness.

How to Make Love More Sacred:

Slow down and be fully present in every touch.

Breathe together. Syncing your breath deepens the connection.

Set an intention before love-making (such as honoring each other's souls, healing, or channeling divine energy).

Use sacred elements (candles, oils, soft lighting) to create a space of reverence. Whisper words of devotion, allowing sound to deepen the energy between you.

Why it works:

Transforms intimacy into a divine experience, not just physical pleasure. Strengthens energetic and emotional bonds.

Opens the heart chakra, creating deeper vulnerability and trust.

6. Spiritual Check-In. Evolving Together with Awareness

Growth is constant, and it's important to stay in tune with each other's spiritual journey.

How to Do a Spiritual Check-In:

1. Set aside sacred time weekly or monthly.

2. Ask deep questions to reflect on where you are spiritually: What are you learning about yourself right now?

How do you feel our love is evolving?

What spiritual practices do we need more of?

3. Celebrate each other's growth and offer support.

Why it works:

Ensures you both are growing together, not apart. Builds deeper understanding and emotional connection.

Keeps the relationship aligned with your shared spiritual vision.

Final Thought:

Love That Grows Spiritually Lasts Eternally A couple that prays together evolves together and nurtures their spiritual bond will never be shaken.

They do not just love each other's. They honor, uplift, and guide each other toward them highest potential.

They do not fear change because they trust in divine timing and growth.

They do not just exist together, they walk a shared spiritual path, leading to something greater than themselves.

This is the kind of love that transcends time, deepens with each lifetime, and reflects the divine in its purest form.

Chapter 22
Strengthening the Sacred Bond While Apart: A Ceremony of Reunion

True love does not weaken with distance. It deepens, strengthens, and intensifies when nurtured with intention. When a spiritually connected couple is apart, they are not separate; they are simply experiencing love in its energetic form rather than physical presence.

The time spent apart should not be filled with longing and emptiness. Still, it should be used to build desire, amplify connection, and prepare for a sacred reunion that is not just about physical pleasure but a ceremonial merging of souls.

This chapter explores how to cultivate feelings of devotion and desire while apart, ensuring that each reunion is a profound, sacred event.

1. The Power of Absence: Why Distance Can Strengthen Love

Love, like fire, needs both closeness and space to burn brightly. When apart, lovers have the opportunity to strengthen their emotional and spiritual connection beyond the physical.

Heighten desire by allowing longing to build naturally.

Prepare for an intentional reunion where love is not just expressed but honored as a sacred force.

A true spiritual connection does not fade with distance. It intensifies in anticipation of returning to oneness.

2. Building Desire & Emotional Intimacy While Apart

Desire is not just about physical attraction; it is about the longing to merge, connect, and exist as one.

Sacred Practices to Strengthen Desire While Apart:

1. The Heart Connection Meditation (Deepening emotional presence even in absence.) Close your eyes and visualize your partner.

Imagine your heartbeats syncing, your energy intertwining, your love surrounding you both like golden light.

Whisper words of longing and devotion into the space between you. End with gratitude for the love that exists beyond time and space.

2. Writing Love Letters or Voice Notes (Keeping emotional intimacy alive.) Express what you miss, what you crave, what you cherish.

Speak or write your deepest feelings, desires, and intentions for when you reunite. Use poetic, intentional language to let your words become a bridge between souls.

3. Carrying Each Other's Essence (Keeping the energetic imprint of your love close.) Wear your partner's scent or keep a piece of their clothing nearby.

Hold onto a symbolic object that represents your bond.

Let these physical reminders strengthen the feeling of their presence, even when they are away.

4. Sending Energy to Each Other (Communicating beyond words.) Before bed, close your eyes and send loving energy to your partner. Imagine them feeling your touch, your breath, your warmth from afar. Trust that your love is felt, even in silence.

By practicing these, desire becomes not just physical longing but spiritual anticipation, a hunger to reunite not just in the body but also in the soul.

3. The Ceremony of Reunion Honoring the Return to Oneness

The moment of reunion should not be rushed or treated as ordinary; it should be a sacred event, a ceremonial merging of two energies that are coming back together.

How to Create a Sacred Reunion Ceremony:

1. Prepare Your Space for Love's Return

Cleanse the space with candles, incense, or essential oils (sandalwood, jasmine, or rose to awaken love energy).

Set an atmosphere that reflects the reverence of the moments, soft lighting, sensual music, fresh sheets, and a space that feels sacred.

2. The Ritual of First Touch (Breaking the separation with intention.) When you first reunite, pause before rushing into a physical connection.

We should look into each other's eyes, absorbing the energy that has built up over time.

183

Hold hands, feel each other's presence, and breathe together, allowing the reunion to be fully felt before it unfolds.

3. Speaking Words of Devotion (Honoring the sacred return.) Before intimacy, whisper affirmations of love, such as:

I have missed you, and now I return to you completely.

Distance only strengthens our bond, and our love is infinite. Our reunion is sacred, and our love is divine.

4. Love-Making as Ceremony (Transforming passion into worship.)

Move with intention, presence, and reverence. This is not just about physical pleasure but about two souls merging once again.

Let touch be slow, intentional, feeling every inch of connection renewed. Breathe in unison, letting the rhythm of your love guide the experience.

5. Closing the Ceremony in Stillness (Sealing the energy of reunion.)

After love-making, remain in each other's arms, in silence, absorbing the fullness of connection that has been restored.

Whisper words of gratitude for the love you share.

By making reunions sacred, love becomes not just a habit but a divine experience, one that is treasured, felt deeply, and honored with the highest respect.

4. The Eternal Connection: Love Beyond Physical Presence

Love that is nurtured beyond the physical realm becomes eternal. A spiritual couple understands that they are never truly apart; they are always connected, always feeling each other, and always part of the same divine frequency.

Even when miles separate you, the bond remains:

In that way, your soul calls to theirs in quiet moments.

In the way you feel their presence in the scent of their skin, the echo of their laughter.

In the way, you close your eyes and know without a doubt that you are theirs, and they are yours.

Time apart does not weaken love. It strengthens it. Each reunion becomes a reminder that love is infinite, timeless, and always returning to itself.

Final Thought: Love That Honors Absence Creates Reunions That Are Sacred Desire that is cultivated intentionally becomes devotion.

Love that is honored in absence becomes unbreakable.

A reunion that is treated as sacred becomes a merging of souls, not just bodies.

Let distance be a time to grow, to feel, to crave, to build anticipation so that when love returns to itself, it is met not just with pleasure but with ceremony, reverence, and the highest form of connection.

Chapter 23
Even Months Apart Can Transform Distance into Deeper Devotion

When apart for months, it can feel like an eternity, or it can be an opportunity to cultivate deeper love, stronger devotion, and heightened intimacy. Time apart is not a loss. It is a test of love's endurance, an invitation to build anticipation, strengthen the bond, and prepare for a reunion that is more sacred than before.

When approached with intention, longing, and spiritual awareness, these months become not just waiting but active preparation for something greater. This love is felt beyond time and space, a reunion that is not just physical but soul-restoring.

This chapter explores how to:

Keep love alive and thriving during months apart.

Build anticipation and desire in ways that deepen the connection.

Prepare for a reunion that is not just about pleasure but a sacred homecoming.

1. Shifting Your Mindset: Love is Not on Pause: Time apart is not a break from love. It is an expansion of love.

See the time apart as sacred preparation, not distance. Recognize that love does not fade when nurtured with intention.

Treat every day as part of the reunion journey, allowing love to build, not weaken.

These months apart are an opportunity to:

Strengthen emotional and spiritual intimacy. Deepen trust and devotion.

Heighten desire, anticipation, and sacred longing.

Instead of feeling separated, see yourselves as two souls traveling toward an inevitable, divine merging.

2. Practices to Maintain a Sacred Bond While Apart

Being apart does not mean being disconnected. These daily and weekly practices will help keep the bond strong, ensuring that when you return to each other, love is more intense, more sacred, and more deeply rooted.

1. The Morning & Night Connection Ritual (Staying aligned through presence.)

Each morning, wake up and take a deep breath, imagining your partner beside you. Whisper: I send you love, warmth, and devotion. At night, before sleeping, please close your eyes and visualize their hand in yours, their breath against your skin, their energy surrounding you.

If possible, share a voice note or short message—a simple "Good morning, my love or I miss you tonight keeps the connection alive.

Why it works: Keeps your partner energetically present, ensuring that love remains active in both mind and body.

2. Love Letters of Longing & Devotion (Writing to keep desire alive.)

Writing allows desire to build in a way that spoken words cannot. Write handwritten letters or poetic messages expressing:

What do you miss about them?

The way your body and soul long for them.

Your visions for the reunion.

Exchange letters at different intervals or save them for the moment of return, allowing the longing to deepen anticipation.

Why it works: Written words hold energy; they become tangible reminders of love that are waiting to be read, felt, and absorbed.

3. The Shared Song Ritual (Using music to bridge distance.) Choose one song that belongs to your love.

Whenever you miss each other, play the song at the same time, allowing it to serve as a portal to each other's essence.

Please close your eyes and let the melody fill the space between you, knowing your partner is feeling it, too.

Why it works: Music creates an emotional and sensory link, making love feel present even in absence.

4. The Energy Merge Meditation (Feeling each other's presence beyond distance.)

Find a quiet space.

Sit with your eyes closed and breathe deeply.

Visualize your partner standing in front of you. Feel their eyes, warmth, and love radiate toward you.

Imagine your energies merging, wrapping around each other in golden light.

Hold this visualization for a few minutes, letting the love be felt beyond space and time.

Why it works: Energy does not know the distance. This practice ensures that love is always flowing between you.

5. The Sensory Connection Ritual (Strengthening desire through memory.) Keep a piece of their scent, clothing, or a meaningful object.

Hold it, breathe it in whenever longing arises.

Let it trigger desire, anticipation, and the feeling of closeness.

Why it works: The brain registers scent and touch as memory, making their presence feel tangible even when apart.

Preparing for the Reunion Turning Passion into Sacred Ceremony Reuniting after months apart should not be rushed. It should be treated as a sacred event, a ceremony of love's return.

1. The Space of Welcome (Setting the stage for divine connection.) Prepare a sacred space for reunion: soft lighting, candles, and warmth.

Cleanse the space with oils or incense to symbolize a fresh, renewed beginning. Let your reunion feel intentional, as though love itself is being honored.

2. The First Touch Ritual (Bridging the gap between longing and presence.) When you first see each other, do not rush into an embrace.

Stand still for a moment. Look into each other's eyes, absorbing the reality of return.

Take a deep breath together, letting your energies realign.

Then, touch gently, slowly, with reverence, letting the months of longing melt into one sacred moment.

3. Love-Making as a Homecoming (Turning passion into spiritual merging.) Move with intention. Slow, deep, reverent.

Breathe together, allowing your bodies to realign naturally. Speak words of devotion before surrendering to passion.

Let the moment be more than just physical; it is a merging of souls that have longed for a reunion.

The Final Thought of Love That Endures Time & Space

Love is not weakened by distance. It is strengthened when nurtured.

Absence creates anticipation, heightens devotion, and prepares the heart for something deeper.

Reunions should not be rushed. They should be honored as a sacred return to oneness.

This love does not fade, does not break, does not weaken.

It is waiting, growing, and becoming more profound with every passing day.

The moment of reunion will not just be a meeting of bodies. It will be a merging of everything you have built while apart.

Would you like to add a personal affirmation or mantra for each day spent apart to reinforce the sacred connection?

Chapter 24
Walking the Divine Path Letting God Reveal Sacred Love

Love is a journey, and sometimes, the road we walk is not the one designed for us but the one we have created for ourselves. There are moments when we believe we are building something beautiful, something lasting, only to step back and see that some pieces don't fit, some truths feel incomplete, and something greater is still calling us forward.

It is in these moments that God reveals what we could not see before. He does not punish us for choosing our way but offers us a loving invitation to see a clearer version of what He has always intended for us.

My actions in writing The Art of Love-Making Through God's Eyes come from this very experience, realizing that love is not just human, not just emotional, but deeply sacred. This book is a reflection of what God has revealed to me about intimacy, connection, and divine union. Every word is guided by the inspiration of knowing His love and the wisdom He gives to show us a love that is higher, purer, and more eternal than what we may have designed for ourselves.

When We Walk a Path of Our Design, there are times when we create a life, a relationship, or a love story without fully knowing if it aligns with divine truth.

We follow desires, emotions, and connections that feel right in the moment.

We put together pieces that seemed to fit, only to later realize they were never part of the masterpiece God intended.

We believe we are in control of our journey, only to wake up one day and feel something missing, something only God can reveal.

This is not failure. This is awakening.

Love is not just something we build; it is something God reveals, refines, and perfects. In His time, God Reveals What is Missing. When we are ready, God steps in, not with judgment but with clarity. He does not say, "You have failed," but instead, "Let me show you something greater. " He does not punish but redirects, refines, and realigns.

He allows us to see through His eyes, to recognize that what we thought was whole was only a part of the divine picture.

If love has ever left you feeling incomplete, it is not because you were unworthy; it is because God was preparing you for something deeper.

The Difference Between Self-Made Love & God-Designed Love.

Not all love is created equal. Some love is made by human hands, emotions, or experiences that shape us but do not complete us.

Then there is sacred love, love that is divinely written, that carries God's fingerprints, and that transforms us into something greater.

Self-Made Love: Built on desire, passion, and personal choices. Requires effort to hold together. Often comes with uncertainty, doubts, and fears. Leaves us feeling that something is missing.

God-Designed Love: Built on divine timing, alignment, and purpose. Flows with ease, even though challenges. Brings peace, clarity, and divine confirmation.

Feels whole, complete, and spiritually fulfilling.

Recognizing sacred love means surrendering our idea of what love should be and allowing God to reveal what love truly is.

4. The Calling to Write This Book: A Journey of Revelation

I did not decide to write The Art of Love-Making Through God's Eyes on my own. It was given to me, placed in my heart as a divine assignment, as something I was meant to share.

This book is not just about physical love. It is about:

Recognizing love as a divine covenant.

Understanding intimacy as a sacred act, not just a physical experience. Learning how love-making is an extension of spiritual connection.

Every chapter, every word, every revelation in this book is guided by the love and wisdom God has shown me.

If you are reading this, it is because you, too, are being called to see love differently, to recognize what is truly sacred, and to step into a love that reflects God's highest intention for you.

The Ritual of Surrender: Letting God Led You to Sacred Love.

Before we can fully experience divine love, we must surrender our ideas of love to God.

How to Perform the Sacred Surrender Ritual:

1. Find a quiet space, close your eyes, and take a deep breath.

2. Reflect on past experiences of love. Where did you try to build love on your own?

3. Ask God to reveal His vision of love for you. Whisper:

   Gods open my eyes to love as You see it.

   Please show me what is true, what is whole, what is sacred.

4. Sit in stillness, allowing divine wisdom to fill your heart.

5. Commit to releasing the past and embracing a love that God leads.

If you have ever felt that something was missing in love, it is because God was waiting for you to recognize what He has always intended for you.

Sacred love is not found. It is revealed.

It is not built by human hands; it is written with divine design.

It does not break because it is held together by something greater than emotion—God Himself.

Let this book be a guide, a revelation, and an invitation to step into love that is not just beautiful but sacred, divine, and eternal.

A Prayer for Recognizing & Receiving Sacred Love

Heavenly Father,

I come before You with an open heart, ready to see love through Your eyes.

I surrender my understanding of love, my past experiences, and my desires to You. Reveal to me the love that You have written for my life, the love that is pure, whole, and divinely aligned. If I have built love by my own hands, not knowing what was truly sacred, I ask for Your wisdom to guide me to something greater. Please show me what is missing, not as a correction, but as an invitation to see more clearly. Let me recognize the difference between love that is temporary and love that is eternal.

Prepare my heart to receive the love You have designed for me. Make me ready to give and receive love in its

highest, most divine form. Let my love be a reflection of
You, patient, true, unshakable. I trust in Your timing, in
Your guidance, and your divine plan. I release all fear,
doubt, and control, And I open myself fully to the sacred
love You have prepared for me.

Amen.

The Final Thought: Self-Growth is the Foundation of Sacred Love

Sacred love is not something you chase. It is something you prepare for, attract, and receive when you are ready.

Use your time alone to strengthen yourself so that when love arrives, you are not searching. You are ready.

Embrace growth because the best relationships are not just about love but about becoming the highest versions of yourselves together.

Trust in divine timing, knowing that every moment of self-development is leading you closer to the love that is already written for you.

Love will come. But first, become the love you seek.

Chapter 25
Filling Your Time with Self-Growth: Becoming Ready for Sacred Love

Love is not just about finding the right person; it is about becoming the right person and preparing your heart, mind, and spirit to receive and sustain divine love. The time spent before love, during distance, or in moments of solitude should not be filled with waiting but with growth, refinement, and transformation.

Sacred love requires a strong foundation, which is first built within you.

This chapter explores:

How to use time apart or single seasons for spiritual and personal growth.

Practices that strengthen your mind, body, and soul, making you a vessel for divine love.

How self-growth ensures that when love arrives, you are fully prepared to receive and honor it.

1. The Purpose of Solitude in Love's Journey

Being alone is not a sign that something is missing; it is an opportunity to become full within yourself so that when love enters, it enhances rather than completes you. Time alone refines you. It allows you to grow without distraction.

It prepares you for the responsibility of love. Sacred love requires commitment, patience, and deep self-awareness.

It strengthens your spiritual foundation. The deeper your relationship with God and yourself, the stronger your future relationship will be.

Rather than longing for love, use this time to create a version of yourself that is truly ready for divine connection.

2. The Three Pillars of Self-Growth

Self-growth should be holistic, nurturing the mind, body, and soul to prepare for sacred love truly.

1. Mind: Expanding Your Awareness

Read books that challenge and inspire you. Learn about love, spirituality, and self- discovery.

Journal daily. Reflect on your growth, your desires, and the lessons you are learning.

Set goals for yourself outside of love. Who are you becoming? What are you working toward?

When you know yourself deeply, a strong mind creates a strong love. You love with clarity and wisdom.

2. Body: Treating Your Vessel as Sacred

Move with intention, exercise, dance, and stretch. Keep your body in tune with your energy. Eat nourishing foods that elevate your well-being.

Practice self-touch with presence. Honor your body, not just in physical ways, but by loving the skin you live in, being gentle with yourself, and recognizing that you are already whole.

Your body is the temple where love will reside. Please treat it with reverence.

3. Soul Strengthening: Your Spiritual Connection

To deepen your relationship with God, spend time in prayer, stillness, and divine reflection.

Meditate and practice self-awareness. Listen to your intuition, and follow your inner guidance.

Engage in creative expression. Write, paint, move, and allow your soul to express itself fully.

A nourished soul creates an unwavering love, one that is not dependent on external validation but thrives in divine connection.

3. Practices to Fill Your Time with Meaning & Purpose

If love is on the horizon, use this time wisely and grow into the highest version of yourself.

1. The Self-Reflection Ritual (Understanding Your Growth Journey)

1. Sit in a quiet space and reflect:

What are my strengths? What areas do I need to grow in? What kind of love do I desire? Am I prepared to give and receive it fully?

2. Write a letter to your future self, describing the person you are becoming.

3. Revisit this letter before entering your next relationship, ensuring you are walking in alignment with your highest self.

2. The Practice of Daily Gratitude & Presence (Finding Joy in the Now)

Every morning, write three things you are grateful for, and this shifts your energy into appreciation rather than longing.

Take time to enjoy your own company. Go on solo dates, explore new places, and experience life deeply.

Recognize that you are whole, even before love arrives.

Love is not about finding someone to complete you; it is about sharing your wholeness with another.

3. The Sacred Mirror Exercise (Preparing for Love by Loving Yourself First)

1. Stand in front of a mirror and look into your own eyes.

2. Speak affirmations aloud:

I am already in love.

I am worthy of divine connection.

I prepare myself for sacred love by loving myself first.

3. Do this daily, reminding yourself that the love you seek must first be cultivated within.

4. Preparing for Sacred Love: Becoming a Vessel for Divine Connection

You do not attract sacred love by seeking it. You attract it by becoming it.

Love in the way you live, in the way you speak, in the way you treat yourself and others.

Be patient; love's timing is divine, and preparation is part of the process.

Trust that every moment of self-growth is bringing you closer to a love that is whole, aligned, and eternal.

5. A Prayer for Self-Growth & Readiness for Sacred Love

Heavenly Father,

I thank You for this season of growth and for the time You have given me to become whole within myself.

I surrender my impatience, my longing, and my need to control love's arrival.

Instead, I ask You to prepare my heart, mind, and spirit for the love You have written for me.

Let me use this time to grow in wisdom, strength, and self-awareness.

Refine me so that when love comes, I may receive it fully, honor it completely, and give of myself with purity and devotion.

Teach me to love myself as You love me to see my worth, to walk in confidence, to recognize that I am already whole.

When the time is right, let sacred love find me, but until then, let me fill my days with purpose, my heart with gratitude, and my soul with divine light.

Amen.

The Final Thought: Self-Growth is the Foundation of Sacred Love

Sacred love is not something you chase. It is something you prepare for, attract, and receive when you are ready.

Use your time alone to strengthen yourself so that when love arrives, you are not searching. You are ready.

Embrace growth because the best relationships are not just about love but about becoming the highest versions of yourselves together.

Trust in divine timing, knowing that every moment of self-development is leading you closer to the love that is already written for you.

Love will come. But first, become the love you seek.

Would you like to add a daily affirmation practice for readers to reinforce their journey of self-growth and divine love?

Chapter 26
Finding Ourselves to Discover Our Purpose: The Path to Pure Bliss

To truly experience love, fulfillment, and divine connection, we must first know ourselves. The journey to sacred love begins with self-discovery, finding our purpose, and aligning our lives with meaning.

When we live with purpose, life gains depth, relationships become richer, and love is experienced with greater intention. Purpose is what makes love more than just an emotion. It transforms it into a force that guides, nourishes and elevates.

This chapter explores:

How self-discovery leads to purpose.

Why living with meaning creates joy, love, and contentment. How aligning with purpose allows us to experience Pure Bliss.

1. Finding Ourselves: The Journey Within

Many seek love, happiness, and fulfillment in external things, yet true joy begins with knowing who we are. Before we can live fully, we must first ask:

Who am I when no one is watching?

What do I long for beyond relationships, success, or material things? What makes my soul feel alive?

The more deeply we understand ourselves, the clearer our purpose becomes. When you know yourself, you no longer search for meaning. You become it.

2. Discovering Purpose: The Foundation of a Fulfilling Life

The purpose is not just about what we do. It is about why we exist, what fuels our souls, and what brings true fulfillment.

A life without purpose feels empty, no matter how much love surrounds us. A life with purpose feels whole, even when we are alone.

Signs You Are Living with Purpose:

You wake up excited for life, even in small ways.

You feel deeply connected to your actions and choices.

You experience joy, even in challenges, because everything has meaning. You are not seeking validation. Your fulfillment comes from within.

Love alone cannot bring fulfillment. Only a life rooted in purpose can sustain true joy.

3. How Purpose Leads to Love, Joy & Contentment

When we live with purpose, our love deepens, not just for a partner, but for life itself. Purpose creates inner peace. A heart that is at peace loves with clarity and devotion.

Purpose fills us with joy. When we love our lives, we radiate energy that attracts the right people and experiences.

Purpose strengthens relationships. Instead of seeking fulfillment in others, we bring fulfillment into love.

This is what leads to Pure Bliss, not fleeting happiness, but a deep, unshakable contentment that lasts.

Love without purpose is longing. Love with purpose is fulfillment.

4. Practices to Align with Purpose & Find Pure Bliss

To experience true love and joy, we must live intentionally.

1. The Reflection Ritual: Uncovering Your Purpose

1. Sit in stillness and breathe deeply.

2. Ask yourself: What lights me up? What moments make me feel alive?

3. Write down three things that bring deep meaning to your life.

4. Set an intention to live in alignment with them daily.

We do not find purpose; we uncover it within ourselves.

2. The Daily Meaning Practice: Living with Intention

Every morning, ask: What can I do today that aligns with my purpose?

Every night, reflect: Did I live with meaning today?

Take small actions daily. A purposeful life is built in small, intentional moments.

Joy is not in what we achieve. It is in how we live each moment.

3. The Bliss Visualization: Aligning with Love & Purpose

1. Close your eyes and visualize your highest self, joyful, fulfilled, radiating love.

2. See yourself living a life of deep purpose. What does it look like? Feel like?

3. Imagine love flowing freely through you as part of your purpose, not separate from it.

4. Affirm:

I am living with purpose.

My life is meaningful, joyful, and full of love.

I attract love because I live in alignment with my highest self.

Bliss is not something we wait for. It is something we create by living in truth.

5. A Prayer for Finding Purpose & Pure Bliss

Heavenly Father,

I seek not just love but a life filled with purpose. Help me uncover the path You have designed for me,

A path that brings joy, meaning, and divine connection.

Let me wake up each day with the intention,

Let my actions reflect the love and purpose You have placed within me.

May I find fulfillment not in what I receive but in how I give, not in who loves me but in how I love.

I trust that in living with purpose, love will find me, that is, walking my divine path will give me pure bliss.

Amen.

The Final Thought: Living on Purpose is the Key to Lasting Love & Happiness. When we find ourselves, we see our purpose.

When we live with purpose, we experience joy. When we live with joy, love flows effortlessly.

This is Pure Bliss, not just happiness, but a life filled with meaning, love, and divine fulfillment.

6. The Daily Practice for Living with Purpose & Pure Bliss

To truly embody purpose and experience Pure Bliss, we must make intentional choices every day. This practice will help you align with your highest self, deepen your sense of meaning, and bring love and joy into your daily life.

The Purpose & Bliss Alignment Practice (10 minutes daily)

1. Begin in Stillness (2 minutes) Sit in a quiet space.

Close your eyes and take three deep breaths.

Let go of distractions and bring your awareness to the present moment.

2. Set Your Daily Purpose (2 minutes)

Ask yourself: What is one thing I can do today that aligns with my purpose?

Your purpose doesn't have to be grand. It can be as simple as showing kindness, creating, or learning something new. Please write it down: Today, I will

3. Affirm Your Alignment (2 minutes)

Speak these affirmations aloud or write them down:

I am walking in my divine purpose.

Everything I do today brings me closer to joy and fulfillment. Love, peace, and purpose flow through me effortlessly.

4. Gratitude Reflection (2 minutes) Write down three things you are grateful for. Gratitude aligns your heart with joy and contentment, reinforcing the feeling of bliss.

5. Close with a Blissful Visualization (2 minutes)

Imagine yourself fully aligned, living with purpose, radiating love and joy. Feel that sense of peace, contentment, and fulfillment filling your body.

Smile, knowing you are already on the path to Pure Bliss. Why This Practice Works:

It trains your mind to seek purpose every day.

It helps you feel gratitude and joy in the present moment.

It aligns your thoughts, actions, and emotions with divine fulfillment.

It reinforces that bliss is not in the future. It is something you create daily.

Final Thought: Joy, Love & Purpose Are Already Within You

You do not need to search for bliss. It is waiting for you in the way you live each day.

Love becomes more meaningful when it is part of a life rooted in purpose.

Pure Bliss is not something you wait for. It is something you cultivate, moment by moment, as you align with your highest self.

Chapter 27
Becoming Your Purpose-Driven, Brightest Self

To live fully, love deeply, and experience Pure Bliss, we must step into our highest, brightest, most purpose-driven selves. This is not about becoming perfect; it is about aligning with who we were always meant to be.

A life filled with purpose is a life filled with light, clarity, and deep fulfillment. When you walk in your purpose, you radiate an unshakable, magnetic, and divinely guided presence.

This chapter explores:

How to activate your purpose-driven self.

What it means to live as your brightest, fullest version.

Practices to strengthen purpose, confidence, and divine alignment.

1. What It Means to Be Your Brightest Self

Your brightest self is not just the happiest version of you; it is the most aligned, fulfilled, and purpose-driven version.

It is who you are when you stop playing small, stop doubting yourself, and start stepping into your divine assignment.

Your brightest self is confident not because of ego but because of deep self-knowing.

Your brightest self does not seek approval because you are walking in divine truth. Your brightest self is magnetic because you radiate pure energy, love, and purpose.

When you become this version of yourself, everything shifts. Your relationships deepen, your love expands, and your entire existence feels more alive.

2. Activating Your Purpose-Driven Self

The purpose is not found; it is activated. It is already within you, waiting to be fully expressed.

To unlock this version of yourself, you must:

Let go of fear. Fear dims your light. Trust that you are worthy of your highest purpose. Stop waiting for the right time. Your time is now. Step into your purpose with boldness.

Do what sets your soul on fire. Your brightest self emerges when you engage in what truly fuels you.

You already have everything within you to be your highest self. The only thing left to do is choose it.

3. The 5 Daily Habits to Step into Your Brightest Self

To fully embody your purpose-driven self, these five daily habits will help you stay aligned with your mission and light.

1. The Morning Intention. Starting the Day with Purpose.

Upon waking, ask. What is my purpose today? How can I bring light into this day? Speak an intention aloud:

I walk in purpose today.

I am becoming the highest version of myself. I radiate love, joy, and divine energy.

Move with intention: Start your day knowing you are stepping into your mission.

2. The Self-Awareness Check: Aligning Actions with Your Purpose

Pause throughout the day and ask: Is what I'm doing right now aligned with my highest self?

If not, adjust and shift your focus back to your purpose.

Living on purpose is not about perfection. It is about constant alignment.

3. The Purpose Journal Tracking Your Growth Each night, write down:

One thing you did that aligned with your purpose. One lesson you learned about yourself.

One way you can improve tomorrow.

When you document your purpose, you deepen your connection to it.

4. The Brightness Practice: Expanding Your Energy & Presence Stand tall, breathe deeply, and visualize yourself radiating light. Smile more, speak with warmth, and move with confidence.

Hold eye contact with people, and be fully present in every interaction. Be the energy that lights up the space you enter.

Your brightest self is not just how you feel; it's how you make others feel in your presence.

5. The Sacred Gratitude Reflection Ending the Day with Purpose Before bed, reflect:

Did I live in alignment with my purpose today? Did I bring light into my day and others' lives?

Express gratitude for the journey of becoming your highest self.

Gratitude keeps you anchored in purpose. When you acknowledge your growth, you invite more expansion.

4. The Power of Living as Your Brightest Self

When you fully step into your purpose-driven self:

You attract divine opportunities, love, and abundance effortlessly. You live each day with joy, confidence, and deep fulfillment.

You inspire others just by being who you were meant to be.

This is not just about self-growth; it is about stepping into the divine role for which you were created.

5. A Prayer for Becoming Your Purpose-Driven, Brightest Self

Heavenly Father,

I no longer wish to live in doubt or hesitation.

I am ready to step into the fullness of who You created me to be.

Let my light shine not for my glory but as a reflection of Your divine love.

Help me walk boldly in my purpose.

Let every action, every word, and every moment align with the highest version of myself.

Remove all fear, doubt, and resistance,

And replace them with confidence, joy, and unwavering faith.

I am ready to live as my brightest, most purpose-driven self.

I trust that in doing so, I will find love, abundance, and a life of deep fulfillment.

Amen.

6. Final Thought: Your Purpose Is Your Light

You are already everything you need to be. Your only task is to step fully into it. Your brightest self is waiting for you to say yes.

When you align with your purpose, life shifts, love deepens, and joy becomes effortless.

Your time is now. Step into your light and become the brightest version of yourself.

Chapter 28
The Power of Belief and Manifesting the Life & Love You Desire

Belief is the foundation of everything we create. What we believe about ourselves, love, and our purpose shapes our reality. If we doubt our worth, we unconsciously block the blessings meant for us. But when we believe fully in love, in abundance, in our divine path, we begin to attract exactly what is meant for us.

To live a life of sacred love, divine purpose, and deep fulfillment, we must learn how to Transform limiting beliefs into empowering truths.

Align our energy with the love and life we desire.

Trust fully in God's timing, knowing that what is meant for us will never be missed.

1. The Relationship Between Belief & Reality

Every experience we have is shaped by what we believe. If we believe love is hard, temporary, or painful, we attract relationships that reinforce that belief. If we think that we are worthy of divine, sacred love, we will recognize it when it arrives.

What you expect, you receive. What you focus on expands.

What you speak becomes your truth.

The shift begins not with the external world but with the beliefs you hold within.

2. Releasing Old Stories & Limiting Beliefs

Many people have subconscious beliefs about love and life that hold them back. These beliefs may come from past relationships, family conditioning, or fear-based thinking.

Reflection Exercise: Identifying & Releasing Old Beliefs

1. Write down any limiting beliefs about love, intimacy, or self-worth. Love never lasts.

    I'm not good enough for deep, unconditional love.

    Success is for others, not for me.

2. Challenge those beliefs:

    Where did I learn this? Is it actually true? What if I chose a new belief?

3. Rewrite the belief into a new truth:

    Love is abundant, and I am fully deserving of it.

    I am worthy of deep, passionate, divine love.

    I am aligned with success, abundance, and purpose.

    Your reality will always mirror the stories you tell yourself. Change your story, and you change your life.

3. The Art of Manifestation Aligning with What You Desire

Manifestation is not just about wishing. It is about aligning your thoughts, actions, and energy with what you want to receive.

The 3-Step Manifestation Process

Step 1: Get Clear on What You Desire

Be specific: What does sacred love feel like? How does divine purpose express itself in your life?

Step 2: Align Your Energy

Feel the emotions of already having what you desire. Act as if it is already yours because, energetically, it is.

Step 3: Surrender & Trust

Release control over how and when things will happen.

Trust that God's timing is perfect.

What you seek is already seeking you. You don't have to chase, align, and receive.

4. Creating a Daily Manifestation Ritual

To shift into deep belief and manifestation mode, practice this daily ritual:

The Morning Manifestation Activation (5-10 Minutes Daily)

1. Breathe deeply & enter a calm state.

2. Visualize the life & love your desire. See it. Feel it. Imagine it as already real.

3. Speak affirmations aloud:

I am divinely guided toward love and purpose. I attract sacred love and divine partnership.

My life is unfolding in perfect harmony.

4. End with gratitude:

Thank You, God, for aligning me with my highest good.

Belief is not just thinking something might happen. It is knowing it is already done.

5. A Prayer for Unshakable Belief & Divine Manifestation

Heavenly Father,

I release all doubt, fear, and hesitation.

I align my heart, my mind, and my soul with Your divine plan *for me. I trust that what is meant for me is already on its way.*

Let me walk in unwavering faith,

Knowing that love, abundance, and purpose are already mine. Let my beliefs reflect my highest truth,

And let my life be a testimony of Your divine power. Amen.

The Final Thought: You Are the Creator of Your Reality. Your beliefs shape your life. Choose them wisely.

You are already aligned with divine love and purpose; you have to recognize it. Trust, believe, and watch as everything unfolds in your favor.

NEXT CHAPTER PREVIEW:

Walking in Divine Timing: Trusting the Unfolding of Love & Life

Chapter 29
Walking in Divine Timing and Trusting the Unfolding of Love & Life

One of the hardest lessons in life is trusting the timing of things we deeply desire. We often want love, success, or clarity now, but divine timing operates beyond our control. Sacred love and purpose do not arrive when we demand them; they come when we are truly ready to receive them.

This chapter explores:

How to surrender control and trust divine timing. Why delays are not denials, but divine preparation.

Practices for staying in alignment while waiting for love and purpose to manifest.

1. The Illusion of Control: Letting Go of the Need to Force Things

It is human nature to want to control outcomes, rush, push, and make things happen. But when we force what is not yet meant for us, we create frustration, resistance, and unnecessary struggle.

Signs You Are Fighting Divine Timing:

Feeling anxious about when love or purpose will manifest. Comparing your journey to others.

Clinging to relationships, jobs, or paths that no longer serve you. Ignoring intuitive signs that tell you to wait or redirect.

Nothing meant for you will ever require force. If it's yours, it will flow.

2. The Truth About Delays: God's Protection & Preparation

When something doesn't happen when or how you want, it's easy to feel like you are being blocked or forgotten. But every delay is divine protection and preparation.

Sometimes, you're being protected from something that isn't aligned. Sometimes, the other person or situation isn't ready yet.

Sometimes, you are being given time to heal, grow, and strengthen before receiving your blessing.

If you could see the full picture, you would realize you are always being guided toward something even greater than what you imagined.

3. The Art of Surrender: Finding Peace While You Wait

To walk in divine timing, you must learn to surrender control and trust the unfolding.

How to Surrender Gracefully:

Affirm daily: trust in God's perfect timing.

Detach from the outcome. Hold your desires with open hands, not clenched fists.

Find joy in the present moment. Happiness does not begin after you receive what you desire. It begins now.

Let go of the need to know how and when. You don't need all the details; you need faith.

True surrender is not passive waiting. It is active trust in the unseen.

4. Practices to Stay Aligned While Waiting for Love & Purpose

While waiting for divine timing to unfold, you can actively prepare yourself to receive what is meant for you.

The Divine Timing Alignment Practice (Daily Ritual)

1. Start the day with gratitude for what already is. I am exactly where I need to be.

Every delay is divine redirection.

2. Meditate on the energy of patience and trust. Breathe in surrender, breathe out control.

3. Write down three ways you can grow while waiting.

What can you do today to become more prepared for love, success, or purpose?

4. Close with a statement of trust.

I surrender all timelines. What is meant for me will never be missed.

The best way to prepare for what you want is to become the person who is ready to receive it.

5. The Beauty of Divine Timing: When Everything Falls into Place

When things finally align, you will realize:

The timing was always perfect.

You were never waiting. You were growing. What arrives is more than what you imagined.

And when love, purpose, and success manifest, you will know this was not by accident. This was divinely designed for you.

What is meant for you will always find you in perfect timing.

6. A Prayer for Trusting Divine Timing

Heavenly Father,

I release my need to control, rush, or force what is not yet ready.

I trust in Your perfect timing, knowing that delays are never denials. I surrender my impatience, my doubts, and my fears,

And I open my heart to the unfolding of Your divine plan.

Please help *me find peace in the present, knowing that I am exactly where I need to be. Prepare me for the blessings You have designed for me,*

And when the time is right, let love, purpose, and abundance flow effortlessly into my life.

Amen.

7. Final Thought: Your Timing is Sacred

You are not behind. You are not forgotten.

You are in divine alignment, exactly where you need to be.

Everything you desire is already written for you. Trust, and let it unfold.

NEXT CHAPTER PREVIEW:

The Power of Stillness: Hearing God's Guidance in Silence

Chapter 30
The Power of Stillness Hearing God's Guidance in Silence

In a world filled with noise, distractions, and constant movement, stillness is a rare and sacred space. Yet, it is in the quiet moments that we hear the deepest truths: God's voice, our intuition, and the whispers of divine guidance.

Stillness is not emptiness. It is where clarity, revelation, and divine wisdom unfold.

This chapter explores:

Why stillness is essential for hearing divine guidance.

How to quiet the mind and open your heart to deeper wisdom. Practices for creating sacred silence in daily life.

1. The Sacredness of Stillness: Why We Need Silence to Hear God

Many people struggle to hear God's voice or feel uncertain about their next steps in life. But

God does not shout over the noise. He speaks in whispers, in stillness, in deep knowing.

Stillness allows you to disconnect from external chaos and reconnect with your inner truth. In silence, your intuition strengthens, and you begin to feel what is truly right for you.

It is in quiet moments that clarity, peace, and divine messages arise.

If you are constantly moving, searching, or filling space with distractions, you may miss the answers that are already within you.

2. How Noise Distracts Us from Divine Wisdom

In modern life, we are always doing, consuming, and reacting.

Social media fills our minds with other people's voices.

Overthinking creates mental noise and confusion.

Busyness prevents us from pausing long enough to receive guidance.

When you are always distracted, there is no space for divine messages to come through.

God is always speaking, but are you still enough to listen?

3. The Practice of Sacred Stillness: Creating Space for Divine Guidance

To hear clearly, we must make room for stillness in our daily lives.

The Sacred Stillness Practice (10 Minutes Daily)

1. Find a quiet place. Sit in a peaceful space with no phone and no distractions.

2. Close your eyes and breathe deeply. Allow your body to relax and your mind to slow down.

3. Ask for divine clarity. Whisper: God, what do You want me to hear today?

4. Do not force an answer. Sit in silence, allowing wisdom to rise naturally.

5. Afterward, write down any thoughts, feelings, or insights that come through.

The more you practice stillness, the clearer your connection to divine wisdom becomes.

4. Hearing God's Voice Recognizing Divine Messages

Many people expect God's guidance to come in loud, dramatic ways. But often, it comes in:

Gentle nudges or feelings in your heart (This is the right path). A sudden moment of peace when thinking about a decision.

Different people or signs repeat a message.

A quiet knowing deep inside you beyond logic, beyond doubt.

Divine messages are always present. We need to be still enough to receive them.

5. The Power of Solitude: Learning to Be Alone with Yourself

Stillness is not just about silence. It is about becoming comfortable with your presence.

Many avoid being alone because they fear:

Their thoughts.

What they may realize about themselves.

The discomfort of facing truth without distraction.

But solitude is where self-discovery, deep healing, and divine connection happen.

The more comfortable you are in solitude, the more at peace you are in the presence of God and yourself.

6. A Prayer for Clarity in Stillness

Heavenly Father,

I release the noise, the distractions, **and** *the need* **always to be** *busy. I open my heart to Your voice, Your wisdom, Your divine guidance.*

Let me find peace in stillness, knowing that clarity comes when I trust.

I was hoping you could help *me to listen, not with my ears, but with my spirit. Let my heart recognize Your whispers,*

And let my soul walk in the direction: You are calling me.

I surrender my need to force answers.

I trust that what I need to know will be revealed in perfect time.

Amen.

7. Final Thoughts: Silence is Where Truth is Found

The answers you seek are already within you. Stillness allows them to rise.

Divine guidance does not always come in a loud voice; it comes in peace, knowing, and quiet revelation.

Trust in the power of silence. It is not empty; it is full of wisdom waiting to be heard.

NEXT CHAPTER PREVIEW:

Sacred Presence: The Art of Being Fully in the Moment

Chapter 31
Sacred Presence The Art of Being Fully in the Moment

In a world that constantly pulls us into past regrets or future anxieties, true peace and connection are found in the present moment.

Presence is not just about being physically there. It is about being fully engaged, fully aware, and fully alive. When we learn to be present, we experience love more deeply, hear divine wisdom more clearly, and feel joy more effortlessly.

This chapter explores:

How presence strengthens the love and spiritual connection. The power of being fully engaged in each moment.

Practices to cultivate sacred presence in daily life.

1. What Does It Mean to Be Truly Present?

Most people are only half-living. Their bodies are in one place, but their minds are elsewhere.

Thinking about the past, regretting, replaying, overanalyzing.

Worrying about the future, stressing over what hasn't happened yet.

Distracted in the present, scrolling, multitasking, never fully engaged.

When we are not present, we miss the beauty, the love, and the divine moments unfolding right now.

Presence is not just about where you are; it's about where your heart, mind, and soul are.

2. The Power of Presence in Love & Relationships

Sacred love thrives on presence. Nothing deepens intimacy more than being fully engaged with your partner in every moment.

When you are present, love flows effortlessly.

When you are present, words become unnecessary. Energy speaks louder. When you are present, your partner feels deeply seen, heard, and held.

Signs You Are Not Present in Love:

You are distracted during conversations.

You are physically together but emotionally disconnected. You are caught up in past mistakes or future fears.

Love is not something we find in the future; it is something we experience fully in the present.

3. How Presence Strengthens Your Spiritual Connection

The greatest spiritual truths are revealed in presence.

God speaks in the now. Peace is found in the now. Love exists only in the now.

When we are fully present, we become More aware of divine signs and messages. More in tune with our intuition.

More connected to God's presence in everyday life.

The present moment is where you meet yourself, meet love, and meet God.

4. Practices for Cultivating Sacred Presence

Learning to be present is a daily practice. Here are simple ways to anchor yourself in the now.

The Sacred Presence Ritual (5-Minute Practice Daily)

1. Pause & Breathe: Close your eyes and take three slow, deep breaths.

2. Feel Your Surroundings: Notice the sensations, the air, the sounds, the space around you.

3. Speak a Presence Affirmation:

   I am fully here, fully aware, fully alive.

   This moment is sacred, and I embrace it fully.

4. Engage with the Now: Whatever you are doing, give it your full attention.

5. The Art of Presence in Love: Deepening Connection with Your Partner

When you are with your partner, make presence a sacred practice.

Put away distractions. Phones, stress, to-do lists, set them aside.

Make eye contact. Look deeply into your partner's eyes, seeing and feeling them.

Listen with your heart. Not just to respond but to understand.

Touch with intention. Let a gentle touch, a held gaze, a slow embrace be sacred.

Love deepens not through time but through the moments when we are fully present with one another.

6. A Prayer for Living in the Present Moment

Heavenly Father,

I surrender my worries of the past and my anxieties of the future. I open my heart fully to this moment, knowing that it is sacred.

Let me experience love, peace, and divine presence in the now. Help me to see the beauty in every breath,

To feel the presence of love in every interaction,

And to walk through life with deep awareness and gratitude.

Amen.

7. Final Thoughts: The Present Moment is the Only One
   That Exists

The past is a memory. The future is a vision. The
present is where life happens. Love, joy, and divine
wisdom are always available in the now.

Presence is the key to sacred love, deep peace, and true
fulfillment.

Be here. Be now. Be fully alive.

NEXT CHAPTER PREVIEW:

The Language of the Soul: Communicating Beyond Words in Love & Spirituality

Chapter 32
The Language of the Soul
Communicating Beyond Words in Love
& Silence

There is a language that exists beyond words, a way of connecting, loving, and understanding that goes deeper than speech.

Love is not just what we say. It is in:

The way we look at each other. The way we touch with presence.

The way we feel the energy between us, even in silence.

In both love and spirituality, the deepest truths are often unspoken. Silence is not emptiness. It is a sacred space where understanding, clarity, and connection take form.

This chapter explores:

How to communicate deeply beyond words. The sacred power of silence in love.

What we gain when we learn to be alone and listen to ourselves.

1. When Words Are Not Needed: Understanding Love Energetically

Many believe communication is about what is said, but the most powerful connection happens without words.

A deep gaze can say more than a thousand words.

A touch filled with presence can heal more than conversation. Energy can be felt across distance, binding two souls together.

If we rely only on words to communicate, we miss the deeper language of love.

Silence is not absence. It is present in its purest form.

2. The Sacred Power of Silence in Love

Silence between two people can feel uncomfortable when love is shallow. But in sacred love, silence is a place of trust, peace, and deep knowing.

Signs You've Reached Soul-Level Connection:

You feel at peace just being in each other's presence.

You don't need constant validation; you know you are loved.

You can sit in silence together, and it feels full, not empty.

When love is real, words become secondary to what the heart already knows.

3. Learning to Be Alone: The Power of Silence Within Yourself

Before we can communicate deeply with others, we must learn to be in deep connection with ourselves.

What Silence Teaches You When You Are Alone:

How to listen to your thoughts without fear. How to hear the whispers of your soul.

How to be at peace without external distractions. How to find clarity, self-love, and deeper intuition.

If you cannot sit in silence with yourself, you will always seek distractions. But when you master solitude, you master your power.

4. The Art of Silent Connection: Practices for Deepening Love Beyond Words

Being silent together does not mean disconnection; it means creating space for something deeper.

The Silent Connection Practice (For Couples & Individuals)

1. Sit together (or alone) in stillness. No phones, no conversation, just presence.

2. Breathe deeply, syncing your energy with your partner (or the space around you).

3. If with a partner, gaze into their eyes for 2 minutes. Let the connection speak without words.

4. If alone, place a hand over your heart. Feel your energy, your presence.

5. Afterward, reflect: What did I feel? What did I understand that words could never express?

The deepest connection is felt, not spoken. Let silence guide you into something sacred.

5. What You Gain in Silence: The Gift of Stillness

When you embrace silence, you gain clarity, self-awareness, and peace.

You learn to hear what your soul is saying.

You stop seeking validation from the outside world.

You feel more connected to love, life, and divine presence.

You realize that true connection doesn't require constant conversation. It requires presence.

The world teaches us to fear silence, but silence is where truth is found.

6. A Prayer for Embracing Silence & Deepening Connection

Heavenly Father,

Teach me to find peace in silence. I want to listen not just with my ears but with my soul. Let me embrace stillness, knowing that love is felt beyond words. Help me to communicate with presence, to connect with others through energy, trust, and sacred knowing. Let me be at peace in my solitude, and let me find divine wisdom in the quiet moments of life.

Amen.

7. Final Thoughts: Silence is the Gateway to Truth

Love does not always need words; it speaks through energy, touch, and presence. Being alone is not loneliness. It is a powerful space for self-discovery.

Silence is not empty. It is where we hear the most profound truths.

Embrace the stillness. Listen deeply. Love beyond words.

NEXT CHAPTER PREVIEW

The Art of Receiving: Opening Yourself to Love, Abundance & Divine Blessings

Chapter 33
Alone with Ourselves Attuning to God in Sacred Solitude

To be truly whole, to love deeply, and to walk in divine purpose, we must first learn to be alone with ourselves, not in loneliness, but in deep spiritual communion with God.

The world teaches us that solitude is something to be avoided and that people, noise, and distractions should always surround us. But in truth, solitude is where we meet God, where we hear His voice most clearly, and where we come to know ourselves truly.

This chapter explores How solitude strengthens our relationship with God.

Why time alone is essential for personal and spiritual growth. Sacred practices for deepening our connection to God in stillness.

1. The Purpose of Solitude: Why Being Alone is a Gift

Many fears being alone because they associate it with emptiness, isolation, or lack. But solitude, when approached with intention, is a divine space for transformation, healing, and clarity.

Solitude allows us to hear God's whispers.

It strips away distractions so we can focus on what truly matters. It helps us understand our purpose, desires, and inner truth.

It deepens self-awareness, making us more aligned with divine energy.

If you never sit in solitude, how will you recognize your soul? How will you hear God speaking?

2. Being Alone Does Not Mean Being Lonely

Many people avoid being alone because they are afraid of their thoughts, emotions, or unresolved wounds.

But solitude is not the same as loneliness.

Loneliness is a feeling of emptiness, disconnection, and longing for external validation. Sacred solitude is a space of fullness in which one connects deeply with oneself and God.

Signs You Need More Solitude:

You feel disconnected from yourself or God.

You constantly seek distractions to avoid silence. You feel emotionally overwhelmed and need clarity. You rely on others for validation and direction.

If you are afraid to be alone, it is a sign that solitude is exactly what you need.

3. The Presence of God in Solitude

Many of God's greatest revelations come when people are alone: Moses heard God's voice in the wilderness.

Jesus went into solitude to pray and receive divine strength.

Prophets and spiritual leaders have always sought silence to hear divine wisdom.

When you allow yourself to be alone with God, free from distractions, you create a sacred space for divine communication.

You will feel His presence in the stillness. You will receive clarity and wisdom.

You will experience peace that cannot be found in external things.

God is always speaking, but we must be still enough to listen.

4. Sacred Practices for Connecting with God in Solitude

If solitude is new to you, here are ways to make it a sacred and enriching experience.

The Divine Solitude Practice (15-30 Minutes Daily)

1. Find a quiet space. No distractions, just stillness.

2. Close your eyes and take slow, deep breaths.

3. Speak a simple prayer:

God, I open my heart to You in this silence.

4. Sit in stillness. There is no need to force thoughts; just be present.

5. Listen. Let your soul absorb whatever message God wants to give you.

6. Journal any thoughts, emotions, or divine insights that come to you.

The more you practice being alone with God, the more clearly you will recognize His presence in every moment of your life.

5. What You Gain in Sacred Solitude

When you learn to embrace being alone, you will:

Discover inner peace that is not dependent on others. Gain clarity on your purpose, emotions, and life direction.

Strengthen your spiritual intuition and ability to recognize God's guidance.

Feel a deeper sense of love, wholeness, and divine connection.

Solitude does not take away from life. It enhances everything you experience.

You are never truly alone when you are in communion with God.

6. A Prayer for Sacred Solitude & Divine Connection

Heavenly Father,

I come to You in stillness, in solitude, in surrender.

Let me not fear being alone, but embrace it as a sacred meeting place with You. Teach me to find peace in silence, to hear Your voice in the quiet,

And to know that even in my solitude, I am never truly alone.

Fill this space with Your presence.

Let me grow in wisdom, clarity, and divine understanding. Make my heart a sanctuary where You dwell,

So that in every moment, alone or with others. I remain deeply connected to You.

Amen.

7. Final Thought: The Power of Being Alone with God

Solitude is not emptiness; it is where we find the fullness of God's presence.

Being alone is not loneliness; it is where we meet ourselves and hear divine truth.

The more comfortable you are in silence, the more you will understand yourself, your path, and your purpose.

Embrace sacred solitude. Let it be a place of healing, clarity, and deep divine connection.

NEXT CHAPTER PREVIEW:

The Alchemy of Transformation: How Solitude & Silence Lead to Spiritual Awakening

Chapter 34
The Alchemy of Transformation How Solitude & Silence Lead to Spiritual Awakening.

Transformation does not happen in noise, distraction, or the constant movement of the world. True spiritual awakening happens in stillness, solitude, and the sacred space where we meet God without interference.

The journey of self-discovery, deep love, and divine alignment requires moments of silent reflection, personal solitude, and surrendering to transformation.

This chapter explores:

How solitude refines and awakens the soul.

Why silence is necessary for deep spiritual transformation.

The power of stillness in shaping love, purpose, and divine connection.

1. The Role of Solitude in Transformation

Every soul must go through a season of solitude, a time of deep inner work, reflection, and surrender.

Moses was alone when he encountered God in the burning bush.

Jesus spent 40 days in the wilderness before stepping into His purpose.

Prophets, mystics, and seekers throughout history have withdrawn into solitude for revelation.

This is because transformation requires shedding, clearing, and renewal, which can only happen when we step away from external influences and go inward.

If you are in a season of solitude, trust that God is working deeply within you.

2. Silence as the Gateway to Spiritual Awakening

Silence is not emptiness. It is where truth rises, where illusions fade, and where God speaks.

Many people fear silence because they are afraid of what they will discover. But in truth, silence is where we find clarity, wisdom, and a deeper relationship with God.

What Happens When You Embrace Silence:

Your mind slows down, allowing divine guidance to flow. You begin to hear the voice of God more clearly.

You shed false beliefs, distractions, and attachments.

You awaken to your true self beyond ego, beyond conditioning.

Silence is not empty. It is full of the wisdom your soul has been waiting for.

3. The Pain & Beauty of Transformation

Spiritual transformation is not always comfortable. It often requires Letting go of old versions of yourself.

Releasing relationships, beliefs, and patterns that no longer serve you. Facing deep emotions that have been buried under distraction.

Many avoid solitude and stillness because transformation demands honesty, surrender, and faith in the future.

But transformation is also:

It is a rebirth, a shedding of the past so you can step into your divine self. A healing restoration of your soul to its purest state.

A preparation aligning you with the love, purpose, and abundance that are meant for you.

Every spiritual awakening begins with solitude. Trust the process; you are prepared for something greater.

4. The Alchemy of Solitude: How to Use Stillness for Deep Spiritual Growth

To fully receive the wisdom, healing, and transformation available in solitude, we must approach it with intention.

The Spiritual Awakening Practice (15-Minute Daily Ritual)

1. Find a Quiet Space: No distractions, just stillness.

2. Close Your Eyes & Breathe Deeply: Allow tension to dissolve.

3. Ask for Divine Guidance: Whisper. God, reveal to me what I need to know.

4. Sit in Silence. No expectations, no forcing. Just listen.

5. Write Down Any Insights: Whatever thoughts, feelings, or revelations arise.

6. End with a Prayer of Trust:

I surrender to this transformation, knowing it is leading me to my highest self.

Your soul already knows the way. Silence is how you let it guide you.

5. Embracing Solitude Without Fear

Many people resist being alone because they fear Feeling lost or uncertain.

Confronting past wounds or emotions. Not knowing what comes next.

But solitude is not a punishment. It is an invitation to awaken.

It is where you meet your true self.

It is where you release everything that is not aligned with your spirit. It is where you prepare for the next chapter of your life.

You are never alone when you are walking with God. Let solitude be your sanctuary, not your fear.

6. A Prayer for Spiritual Transformation in Solitude

Heavenly Father,

I surrender to this season of stillness,

Knowing that transformation is happening within me.

Let solitude refine me, renew me, and reveal what I need to know.

Help me to trust in the process,

Even when it feels uncertain, even when I cannot yet see the path ahead. Let me hear Your voice in the silence,

And let me emerge from this time stronger, wiser, and more aligned with my divine purpose.

Amen.

7. Final Thought: Transformation Requires Stillness

You are not alone in your solitude. God is working within you.

Silence is not emptiness; it is full of divine wisdom that is waiting to be received.

Trust the alchemy of transformation. This season is preparing you for your next awakening.

Embrace the stillness. Let it refine you. The next version of you is being born in this silence.

NEXT CHAPTER PREVIEW

The Sacred Covenant of Love: Returning to God's Vision for Divine Union

Chapter 35
The Sacred Covenant of Love—
Returning to God's Vision for Divine
Union

Love, in its purest form, is not just an emotion, a connection, or a choice—it is a covenant. A sacred promise, a divine commitment that mirrors the eternal love God has for His creation.

Modern relationships often focus on passion, convenience, or personal fulfillment, but in

God's design, love is about oneness, sacrifice, and an unbreakable spiritual bond.

This chapter explores:

- What it means to enter a divine covenant in love.

- How sacred love is different from ordinary relationships.

- The steps to aligning your relationship with God's vision.

1. Love as a Covenant, Not Just a Commitment

The world views love as a feeling—something that changes with time, circumstances, or personal desire. But in God's eyes, love is a covenant, a sacred agreement between two souls and Him.

✓ A covenant is unshakable—rooted in divine purpose, not fleeting emotions.

✓ A covenant requires faithfulness—not just in actions, but in heart and spirit.

✓ A covenant is a reflection of God's eternal love—not selfish, but self-giving.

"I will betroth you to Me forever; I will betroth you in righteousness and justice, in love and compassion." Hosea 2:19

When love is built on a divine foundation, it becomes more than an earthly connection—it becomes a spiritual force that withstands all storms.

2. The Difference Between Sacred Love & Worldly Love

To understand the sacred covenant of love, we must recognize how it differs from what the world defines as love.

Worldly Love, Sacred Love

Based on emotions, attraction, and convenience. Rooted in divine alignment, purpose, and commitment. Fades when challenges arise.

Strengthens through trials because God is the foundation. Seeks self-fulfillment first.

Seeks oneness, unity, and giving of oneself. Conditional—depends on what one receives. Unconditional—flows freely as a reflection of God's love.

Sacred love is not about perfection—it is about divine alignment. It is not about avoiding difficulties but about choosing to walk through them together with God.

Love is not just something you find—it is something you build with faith, devotion, and divine guidance.

3. Steps to Aligning Love with God's Vision

To enter a sacred covenant of love, both partners must be willing to:

✓ Put God at the Center – Love cannot be sustained by human effort alone. It must be rooted in God's presence, wisdom, and purpose.

✓ Honor the Relationship as Sacred – Treat love as a spiritual commitment, not just an emotional connection.

✓ Practice Selfless Love – Love is not about taking—it is about giving, nurturing, and supporting one another's highest self.

✓ Commit to Growth Together – A divine relationship is a journey of constant transformation.

Love in its truest form is not about what we get—it is about what we give and how we reflect God's love through our actions.

4. The Sacred Union Ceremony—A Private Covenant with God

If you and your partner desire to align your love with God's vision, you can perform a sacred union ceremony— a moment of prayer and commitment before God.

📖 The Sacred Covenant Ritual (For Couples)

1. Create a Sacred Space – Light candles, play soft instrumental music, and enter the moment with reverence.

2. Pray Together:

- Thank God for the love you share.

- Ask for divine guidance, protection, and strength in your union.

3. Speak Your Covenant to One Another:

- "I commit to loving you in faith, truth, and divine purpose."

- "I promise to walk this path with you, with God as our guide."

Seal the Moment in Silence or Embrace – Absorb the energy of this promise, letting God's presence fill the space.

A sacred covenant is not just about words—it is about intention, devotion, and a lifelong commitment to love as God designed.

4. A Prayer for Entering the Covenant of Divine Love

Heavenly Father,

Let this love be a reflection of Your eternal covenant—Pure, unshakable, and filled with divine purpose.

May we love as You love,

Not just in passion but in patience. Not just in joy but in faithfulness.

Not just in words but in unwavering devotion.

Let our love be a testimony of Your presence, A bond that cannot be broken,

A light that guides others to see what love was always meant to be.

Amen.

5. Final Thought—Love is a Divine Promise

- Love is not just about connection—it is about divine commitment.

- When love is a covenant, it is unshakable, unwavering, and eternal.

- God's vision for love is not fleeting—it is a reflection of His infinite devotion to us.

When two souls come together in sacred union, with God as their foundation, love becomes more than human—it becomes divine.

NEXT CHAPTER PREVIEW:

The Divine Reflection—How Love Teaches Us About God & Ourselves

Chapter 36
The Divine Reflection—How Love Teaches Us About God & Ourselves

Love is more than an experience—it is a mirror. Every relationship, every connection, every sacred bond reflects something deeper within us. Through love, we learn who we are, who we are becoming, and how God's presence is woven into our very existence.

Love is a teacher, revealing:

- Our capacity to give and receive love.

- The hidden wounds and fears that still need healing.

- The nature of God's love and how it transforms us.

This chapter explores:

- How relationships serve as mirrors for spiritual growth.

- The ways love reflects both our strengths and our wounds.

- How love ultimately brings us closer to understanding God.

1. Love as a Mirror—Seeing Ourselves Through Connection

Love is not just about what we feel—it is about what we see within ourselves through the presence of another.

✓ A healthy relationship reflects our highest potential.

265

✓ A difficult relationship reveals our deepest wounds.

✓ Every love story is an opportunity for transformation.

The relationships we attract often mirror our inner world. If we have unresolved wounds, we may attract partners who expose them—not to harm us, but to help us heal and grow.

Love is always teaching—showing us both the beauty and the shadows within ourselves.

2. Love as a Reflection of God's Love

God's love is the purest, most unconditional love—and our relationships are meant to reflect that divine love.

✓ When we love with patience, we reflect God's patience.

✓ When we love with forgiveness, we mirror God's grace.

✓ When we love without expectation, we embody God's unconditional love.

But love also reveals where we fall short.

• Do we love only when it's easy?

• Do we hold on to resentment instead of offering grace?

• Do we give love freely, or do we guard our hearts in fear?

Every act of love is an opportunity to align ourselves more deeply with God's nature.

3. The Wounds Love Reveals—Healing Through Connection

Not all reflections are easy to face. Sometimes, love exposes pain, insecurities, or fears we have buried deep inside.

Common Emotional & Spiritual Wounds Love Reveals:

✓ Fear of abandonment – Do you cling too tightly out of fear of loss?

✓ Fear of vulnerability – Do you struggle to trust and let someone in?

✓ Self-worth struggles – Do you feel unworthy of deep love?

✓ Past trauma – Are you carrying old wounds into new relationships?

Instead of seeing these as signs of brokenness, we must see them as invitations to heal.

✓ Love does not cause wounds—it reveals what is already inside so we can bring it to the surface and surrender it to God for healing.

If love exposes pain, it is not to harm you—it is to free you.

4. The Reflection of Love in Action—How We Show Up in Love

If love is a mirror, then how we love others is also a reflection of our spiritual journey.

🪶 Self-Reflection Exercise: What Is Love Teaching You?

Ask yourself:

1. How do I give love?

- With patience or with expectation?

- With trust or with fear?

2. How do I receive love?

- With gratitude or with doubt?

- With openness or with hesitation?

3. What is love revealing about my spiritual growth?

- Where am I reflecting God's love?

- Where do I still need healing and transformation?

Love is always a teacher—showing us where we are and where we are called to grow.

5. How Love Brings Us Closer to God

At its highest level, love is a pathway to God. It teaches us:

✔ How to surrender control – True love requires trust, just as faith does.

✔ How to love beyond ego – Love calls us to selflessness, just as God loves us unconditionally.

✓ How to let go and trust divine timing – Love cannot be forced; just as spiritual growth unfolds in divine order.

When we embrace love as a spiritual journey rather than just an emotional experience, we begin to see it for what it truly is—a divine reflection of God's nature within us.

The more we learn to love, the closer we come to understanding the heart of God.

6. A Prayer for Seeing Love Through God's Eyes

Heavenly Father,

Thank You for the gift of love—

A reflection of Your presence, a path to deeper understanding.

Help me to see love as You do—

Not as something to possess but as something to give freely. Not as something to control but as something to surrender to.

Not as something to seek externally but as something to cultivate within.

Let every relationship be a mirror of Your truth, A space of healing, a journey of growth,

A sacred reminder that love is always leading me closer to You. Amen.

7. Final Thought—Love as a Divine Reflection

- Love is a mirror—showing us who we are, where we need healing, and how we are growing.

- Through love, we see both our deepest wounds and our highest potential.

- When we embrace love fully, we begin to understand the depth of God's love for us.

Love is not just an experience—it is a spiritual reflection, a sacred teacher, a pathway to divine awakening.

NEXT CHAPTER PREVIEW:

The Eternal Dance—Love as a Lifelong Journey of Surrender & Becoming

Chapter 37
The Eternal Dance—Love as a Life long Journey of Surrender & Becoming

Love is not a destination—it is a journey, a dance, an unfolding. It is not something we attain once and hold onto, but something we constantly surrender to, evolve with and allow to shape us.

In every season of love—whether in romance, friendship, or divine connection—we are invited to:

✓ Surrender to what love is teaching us.

✓ Evolve into higher versions of ourselves.

✓ Embrace love as a lifelong practice of giving, receiving, and becoming.

This chapter explores:

• Why love is an ongoing journey of transformation.

• How surrendering to love deepens our spiritual growth.

• The sacred balance between holding love and letting it flow freely.

1. Love is Always Changing—So Must We

Many people think love is something to attain and keep static. But love, like life, is fluid, dynamic, and constantly changing.

✓ Love in its highest form is not stagnant—it grows, deepens, expands.

✓ True love requires movement, adaptation, and willingness to transform.

✓ Every stage of love invites us to become more of who we are meant to be.

"Love is like the ocean—sometimes calm, sometimes wild, but always in motion."

To truly experience love, we must release our grip on control and surrender to the rhythm of its flow.

2. The Dance of Surrender—Letting Go & Trusting Love's Path

Surrender is one of the greatest lessons loves teaches us.

✓ Surrendering does not mean giving up—it means trusting.

✓ Surrendering means letting love unfold in divine timing, not forcing outcomes.

✓ Surrendering allows love to move through us freely, without fear or resistance.

Where does love call you to surrender?

• Are you trying to control love instead of letting it breathe?

• Are you afraid to be vulnerable, to trust fully?

- Are you holding onto a past version of love instead of embracing what it is now?

Love, like a dance, requires both leading and surrendering, moving and allowing.

3. Becoming Through Love—How Love Transforms Us Over Time

Love is not just something we experience—it is something that shapes us.

✓ It teaches patience, understanding, and selflessness.

✓ It reveals where we are still growing, healing, and evolving.

✓ It calls us into deeper versions of ourselves.

Each season of love transforms us:

- The first love teaches us innocence, excitement, and wonder.

- The heartbreaks teach us resilience, self-worth, and healing.

The deep, lasting love teaches us devotion, commitment, and the power of choosing love daily.

We do not love the same at 20 as we do at 40. And that is the beauty of it—love evolves, and so do we.

4. Holding Love & Letting Love Flow—The Divine Balance

One of the greatest struggles in love is learning when to hold on and when to let go.

✓ We must hold love gently, not with fear but with gratitude.

✓ We must allow love to flow, trusting that what is meant for us will always remain.

✓ We must not cling to love in fear of loss but embrace love in the fullness of its presence.

What love asks of us:

- Hold space for it, but do not imprison it.

- Nurture it, but do not suffocate it.

- Let it grow, even when growth requires change.

Love is most powerful when it is allowed to move freely, unforced and unbound.

5. The Lifelong Practice of Love—Living in the Energy of Love Daily

Love is not just an emotion—it is a daily choice, a state of being, a way of existing.

How to live in the energy of love daily:

✓ Love yourself first. You cannot pour from an empty cup.

✓ Give love freely, without expectation. Love is not a transaction—it is an offering.

✓ Receive love fully. Let yourself be loved as deeply as you love others.

✓ Trust love's process. Even when it shifts, even when it evolves, even when it asks you to surrender.

Love is not just something we experience—it is something we embody every single day.

Chapter 38
When Frequency of Lovemaking Becomes A Divine Exchange of Energy

Lovemaking, when aligned with truth, love, and spiritual connection, is more than a physical act, it is an energetic exchange, a merging of frequencies, a divine resonance between two souls.

At its highest form, it is not just about pleasure but about the attunement of two beings harmonizing, vibrating at the same rhythm, creating something beyond themselves.

1. The Frequency of Desire, Magnetism and Pull

Before bodies touch, energy is already moving.

The air between two lovers becomes charged, electric, and alive.

The anticipation is not just physical. It is a call from one soul to another.

Their frequencies begin to sync, drawn together like magnets seeking alignment.

2. The Frequency of Presence. Being Fully in the Now

True lovemaking exists in the present moment, where time dissolves.

When two people are fully present with each other, their energy fields merge. Thoughts fade, and only sensation, connection, and breath remain.

This is where frequencies begin to amplify, where two separate beings begin to move as one.

3. The Frequency of the Body, Rhythm, Touch, and Flow

Bodies are instruments playing a song that is both instinctual and deeply intentional. Heartbeats synchronize.

Breath aligns.

Movements become waves, a dance of giving and receiving, push and pull, rise and fall. The body holds memory, and in this moment, it speaks without words.

4. The Frequency of Emotion. Love as an Energy Field

When love is present, the frequency shifts from pleasure alone to sacred intimacy. The body is not just touched. The soul is held.

The experience is not just about release. It is about depth, surrender, and trust.

The more love there is, the higher the vibration, turning something physical into something divine.

5. The Frequency of the Spirit. Sacred Union

At its highest form, lovemaking becomes a prayer, a merging of spirits.

It is no longer about just two people; it is about something greater moving through them. A divine presence enters the space.

The pleasure, the closeness, the intensity all of it is a reflection of the way the universe was created.

The two become one flesh, one energy, one creation.

6. The Frequency of Afterglow. Echoes of Connection

After the merging, the frequency does not fade. It lingers.

The body remains warm, still carrying the energy of what was shared. The souls remain tethered, even when they part.

The connection is not lost. It has left an imprint, a ripple in both beings.

Lovemaking, at its highest frequency, is a language of the soul.

It is more than touch, more than pleasure, it is energy, it is exchange, it is creation.

A Prayer for Surrendering to Love's Journey

Heavenly Father,

Let me surrender to love—

To its lessons, its transformations, its unfolding path.

Help me release control, trusting that love will guide me where I am meant to be. Let me love without fear, without conditions, without resistance.

Let me hold love gently, nurturing it but never trapping it.

Let me become more of who I am meant to be through love's lessons.

I surrender to love's eternal dance,

And I trust that it will always lead me to You. Amen.

7. Final Thought—Love is a Dance, not a Destination

- Love is always changing, always teaching, always calling us to evolve.

- Surrendering to love allows it to move through us freely, without fear.

- Love, in its truest form, is a journey of constant becoming.

Let love be your dance. Let love be your teacher. Let love lead your home.

Acknowledgment & Gratitude

I would like to thank God and Life itself for giving me the passion and the calling to write this book. This journey has not been just about words on a page—it has been a spiritual unfolding, a revelation of divine love, and a deep remembrance of what sacred intimacy truly means.

I am eternally grateful for God's love, His wisdom, and the guidance He has placed in my heart. Through every lesson I have endured in my life, I have come to see that nothing is wasted—every experience, every trial, every moment of joy and pain has been shaping me, preparing me to understand and share this wisdom.

More than anything, I have learned that our connection to God must be woven into every aspect of our lives—not just in times of need but in every decision, every relationship, and every path we walk. And this is something we must pass down to our children—the understanding that life has meaning when it is lived in alignment with God.

Let us teach our children from a young age to move through life with God's voice in their hearts. Let us encourage them to ask for direction in everything they do—to seek God's wisdom when choosing their friends, their path, their education, their careers, and, most importantly, their life partners.

A foundation built on God's guidance is a foundation that will stand through all seasons of life. It will shape the way they love, the way they grow, and the way they experience the sacredness of relationships. With this solid structure, life holds true meaning—a meaning that will not fade but will endure for a lifetime.

I am honored to have written this book, and I pray that its words serve as a light, a guide, and a reminder that love, in its highest and purest form, is always rooted in the divine.

May this book bless you, teach you, and draw you closer to the sacred art of love-making through God's eyes.

With gratitude and love, Olga Tomaszewski

"The best and most beautiful
things in the world cannot be seen
or even touched – they must be
felt with the heart." —Helen Keller.

www.ingramcontent.com/pod-product-compliance
Lightning Source LLC
Chambersburg PA
CBHW051135120626
46547CB00012B/818